Hettner-Lectures

Series editors:
Hans Gebhardt and
Peter Meusburger

Managing editor:
Michael Hoyler

Volume 7

Department of Geography
University of Heidelberg

Institutions, Incentives and Communication in Economic Geography

Hettner-Lecture 2003
with
Michael Storper

Franz Steiner Verlag 2004

Bibliografische Information der Deutschen Bibliothek
Die Deutsche Bibliothek verzeichnet diese Publikation
in der Deutschen Nationalbibliografie; detaillierte
bibliografische Daten sind im Internet über
<http://dnb.ddb.de> abrufbar.

ISBN 3-515-08453-3

ISO 9706

Jede Verwertung des Werkes außerhalb der
Grenzen des Urheberrechtsgesetzes ist unzulässig
und strafbar. Dies gilt insbesondere für Übersetzung,
Nachdruck, Mikroverfilmung oder vergleichbare
Verfahren sowie für die Speicherung in Datenver-
arbeitungsanlagen. © 2004 by Franz Steiner Verlag
Wiesbaden GmbH, Sitz Stuttgart. Gedruckt auf
säurefreiem, alterungsbeständigem Papier.
Druck: Printservice Decker & Bokor, München
Printed in Germany

Contents

Introduction: Hettner-Lecture 2003 in Heidelberg   3
PETER MEUSBURGER and HANS GEBHARDT

Society, community and economic development   7
MICHAEL STORPER

Buzz: face-to-face contact and the urban economy   43
MICHAEL STORPER and ANTHONY J. VENABLES

Technology, organization, territory: a biographical interview with Michael Storper   69
MICHAEL HOYLER, TIM FREYTAG and HEIKE JÖNS

The Klaus Tschira Foundation gGmbH   87

Photographic representations: Hettner-Lecture 2003   91

List of participants   101

INTRODUCTION

Introduction: Hettner-Lecture 2003 in Heidelberg

PETER MEUSBURGER and HANS GEBHARDT

The Department of Geography, University of Heidelberg, held its seventh 'Hettner-Lecture' from June 23-27, 2003. This annual lecture series, named after Alfred Hettner, Professor of Geography in Heidelberg from 1899 to 1928 and one of the most reputable German geographers of his day, is devoted to new theoretical developments in the crossover fields of geography, economics, the social sciences, and the humanities.

During their stay, the invited guest-speakers present two public lectures, one of which is transmitted via teleteaching on the Internet. In addition, several seminars give graduate students and young researchers the opportunity to meet and converse with an internationally acclaimed scholar. Such an experience at an early stage in the academic career opens up new perspectives for research and encourages critical reflections on current theoretical debates and geographical practice.

The seventh Hettner-Lecture was given by the internationally leading economic geographer Michael Storper, Professor of Economic Sociology, Institut d'Etudes Politiques de Paris ("Sciences Po"), Centennial Professor of Economic Geography, London School of Economics and Political Science, and Professor of Regional and International Development, University of California, Los Angeles. Michael Storper's research focuses on theories and processes of regional development. He is widely known for his work on the role of untraded, 'relational' factors for the geographical concentration of economic activities. Storper has also investigated the effects of liberalised trade and technology flows on global industrial location patterns and is interested in different pathways to globalization and resulting developmental inequalities between regions. His books include *Production, work, territory: the geographical anatomy of industrial capitalism* (edited with Allen Scott, 1986), *The capitalist imperative: territory, technology and industrial growth* (with Richard Walker, 1989), *Pathways to industrialization and regional development* (edited with Allen Scott, 1992), *Worlds of production: the action frameworks of the economy* (with Robert Salais, 1997), *The regional world: territorial development in a global economy* (1997), and *Latecomers in the global economy* (edited with Tavros Thomadakis and Lena Tsipouri, 1998).

During the Hettner-Lecture 2003 Michael Storper presented two public lectures entitled 'Society, community and economic development: why some places keep developing and others become blocked' and 'Buzz: face-to-face contact and the urban economy',[1] both of which are published here in revised form, together with a

---

[1] 'Society, community and economic development: why some places keep developing and others become blocked', *Alte Aula der Universität*, Monday, 23rd June 2003, 18.15; afterwards reception.

biographical interview and a short photographic documentation. Three seminars with graduate students and young researchers from Heidelberg and thirteen other European universities took up issues raised in the lectures. The seminars were entitled 'Society, community and economic development', 'Face-to-face contact and the urban economy', and 'Economic geography and the mirage of the cultural turn'.

We should like to express our gratitude to the *Klaus Tschira Foundation* for generously supporting the Hettner-Lecture. Particular thanks are due to Dr. h.c. Klaus Tschira for his continuing interest in cutting-edge geographical research.

The Hettner-Lecture 2003 would not have been possible without the full commitment of all involved students and faculty members. Once again, Tim Freytag, Michael Hoyler and Heike Jöns were crucial in all organisational and conceptual matters. We are also grateful to the students who helped with the organisation of the event. The concerted effort and enthusiasm of all participants once more ensured a successful Hettner-Lecture in Heidelberg.

'Buzz: face-to-face contact and the urban economy', *Hörsaal des Geographischen Instituts*, Tuesday, 24th June 2003, 15.15.

SOCIETY, COMMUNITY AND ECONOMIC DEVELOPMENT

Society, community and economic development[*]

MICHAEL STORPER

0. Society or community?

California's Silicon Valley, the heart of the world's microelectronics and internet industries, is described by some analysts as a tightly-woven community, whose economic performance depends on informal networks of entrepreneurs and techno-nerds.[1] But by others it is described as a set of overlapping markets, with research universities, government financing, venture capitalists, law firms, stock options, high labor mobility, brutal competition, and "accountability" (reputation) rather than trust underlying its business networks.[2] In the latter version, Silicon Valley takes American commercial culture to its limits; in the former, it is a high-technology version of the networked entrepreneurialism and strong social capital commonly associated with European small-firm clusters.[3] Is it society that leads to success, or is it community?

Failure stories in the economic development literature share this ambivalence. We frequently hear criticisms (in the Western press, at least) of "crony capitalism" in Asia. Family-based production networks – certainly a form of cronyism – work well in Taiwan, and are often cited as one aspect of the "good" communitarian structures

---

[*] Earlier versions of this paper were presented to the Third International Seminar of the University of São Paulo, Faculties of Economics and Sociology, October 2002, to the SPURS Geography of Innovation Seminar at MIT, February 2003, and to the NOLD Doctoral School in Tromsø, Norway, April 2003. The field research which stimulated this paper was carried out jointly with Lena Lavinas (Federal University of Rio de Janeiro), in a project financed principally by the Banco do Nordeste Brasileiro (BNB). Thanks also go to the Brasilian Econometrics Society for administration of the funds. Additional financial support came from the William and Flora Hewlett Foundation and the UCLA Center for Latin American Studies. Logistical support was provided by UCLA, the Instituto de Pesquisa Econômica Aplicada (IPEA), Rio de Janeiro, and the Center for Research on Territories, Technologies and Society (LATTS) at the Ecole Nationale des Ponts et Chaussées, France. The views expressed in this paper are exclusively those of the author and not of any of these institutions. Special thanks are due to Eduardo Garcia, the chief research assistant to Lena Lavinas throughout this project, for his extraordinary intellectual and logistical contributions to the research. Additional research assistance was provided by Yun-chung Chen, PhD candidate at UCLA. I also wish to thank my LSE colleague Andrés Rodríguez-Pose for his detailed and insightful comments, and especially for Figure 5.

[1] AnnaLee Saxenian, *Regional advantage: culture and competition in Silicon Valley and Route 128* (Cambridge, MA: Harvard University Press, 1994).

[2] Stephen Cohen and Gary Fields, 'Social capital and capital gains in Silicon Valley', *California Management Review* 41 (1999) pp. 108-30.

[3] Michael J. Piore and Charles F. Sabel, *The second industrial divide: possibilities for prosperity* (New York: Basic Books, 1984).

found in the Third Italy, but they are deplored when they become clannish, as in the Mezzogiorno.[4] In the garment, toy, and jewelry industries in Los Angeles, by contrast, ethnic and family networks of small firms do not seem to lead to long-term development, but rather to lock-in to a vicious circle of cheap products, very low wages, and Third World competition.[5] France has been viewed by some economic historians as owing her successes in economic modernization to a strong State which had the strength to "tame" strongly localist, family-oriented capitalism: society triumphed over community by neutralizing the latter.[6] But others complain that this same State has left an institutional void, with weak spontaneous associational capacities – i.e. weak communities – making it impossible for France to have a vibrant entrepreneurial economy.[7]

Underlying these debates is the classical sociological question of society and community as different types of social order – rule-bound and anonymous exchanges between individuals versus customary social bonds within groups – via which social life gets organized. In place of this pitched debate between partisans of society or community as key to development, we shall argue that both societal and communitarian bonds between economic agents shape long-term economic development, and it is the specific nature of their interrelations that matters.

To consider the importance of societal and communitarian forces to economic development is to think about institutions. "Institutions" refers not only to the formal private and public sector organizations and rules which influence how agents interact, but also to the relatively stable collective routines, habits, or conventions that can be observed in any economy. Institutions have many functions, including the redistribution of wealth, definition of property rights, governance of firms and labor relations, the rule of law, and resolution of disputes. These kinds of institutions vary greatly among countries and have significant impacts on economic performance and socio-economic structures.

---

[4] Diego Gambetta (ed.) *Trust: making and breaking cooperative relations* (Oxford: Blackwell, 1988); Robert Leonardi, 'Regional development in Italy, social capital, and the Mezzogiorno', *Oxford Review of Economic Policy* 11 (1995) pp. 165-79.

[5] Allen J. Scott, *Technopolis: high-technology industry and regional development in Southern California* (Berkeley: University of California Press, 1993).

[6] Pierre Grémion, *Le pouvoir périphérique: bureaucrates et notables dans le système politique français* (Paris: Editions du Seuil, 1976); Richard F. Kuisel, *Le capitalisme et l'Etat en France: modernisation et dirigisme au XXe siècle* (Paris: Gallimard, 1984).

[7] Paul D. Reynolds, S. Michael Camp, William D. Bygrave, Erkko Autio and Michael Hay, *Global entrepreneurship monitor; 2001 executive report* (Kansas City, MO: Kauffman Center for Entrepreneurial Leadership at the Ewing Marion Kauffman Foundation, 2001); Jonah Levy, *Tocqueville's revenge: state, society and community in contemporary France* (Cambridge, MA: Harvard University Press, 1999); Pierre Rosenvallon, *Le modèle politique français* (Paris: Editions du Seuil, 2004).

The argument of this paper is that relations between societal and communitarian forces shape these institutions. They do this by shaping the conventional forms by which individuals can participate and interact in the economy. It then argues that these patterns of participation and their associated incentives critically affect the amount of long-term economic development which takes place, as well as the evolutionary self-selection of economies into particular mixtures of strengths and weaknesses.

1. What do we mean by society and community?

Sociologists invented the analytical distinction between community and society as a way of considering different forms of social integration. A century later, most theories of the "social foundations of development" still rely on the fundamental concepts of sociology – *Gemeinschaft* (community), and *Gesellschaft* (society) – derived from the classical formulations of Weber and Tönnies, or from Durkheim's cognate notion that there are two different kinds of bond between people, *solidarité mécanique* and *solidarité organique*.[8] These distinctions have largely been retained, with "community" conventionally used to refer to forms of collective life in which people are tied together through tradition, interpersonal contacts, informal relationships, and particularistic affinities, interests or similarities, while "society" generally refers to collectivities held together through anonymous, rule-bound, more transparent, formal, and universalistic principles.

From the late 19th to mid-20th centuries, sociologists for the most part fell into line with the other social sciences in seeing community largely as an obstacle to modernization.[9] Starting with Max Weber, community was held to be inimical to the expansion of formal, distanced, rule-bound, transparent social linkages, necessary for achievement of a successful market economy and industrial society.[10] This idea is strongly compatible with formal notions in contemporary economics and political science that communities are groups which engage in rent-seeking and are beset by principal-agent problems for their members; hence, they reduce both freedom and efficiency.[11]

---

[8] Emile Durkheim, *The division of labor in society* (1893), translated by W.D. Halls (New York: The Free Press, 1984).

[9] Although Le Play and others from certain European historical schools were dissenters to this general trend.

[10] Max Weber, *Economy and society* (1921), edited by Guenther Roth and Claus Wittich (New York: Bedminster Press, 1968).

[11] Mancur Olson, *The logic of collective action* (Cambridge, MA: Harvard University Press, 1965); James Buchanan and Gordon Tullock, *The calculus of consent* (Ann Arbor: University of Michigan Press, 1962).

From Durkheim onward, there have also been opposite fears, that too much society and too little community could be problematic to individuals, if not for societal development itself. From the 1940s through the 1960s, there were regular warnings to social science about the importance of community, and not merely its dysfunctional progress-blocking nature.[12] Daniel Bell, among the most prominent of these voices, warned about alienation and excessive anonymity, rekindling old Durkheimian themes.[13] There is today a debate as to whether large-scale, rational, bureaucratic principles – along with the individualization, ephemerality, and mobility they seem to call forth – have not gone too far, weakening forms of community necessary to social order.[14] Among the many concepts deployed in the contemporary debate are "social capital"[15]; "civil society"[16]; "hypermodernity"[17], and a wide variety of reflections on the recrudescence of religious, spiritual and identity politics in the advanced countries.[18]

This type of reasoning has also become centrally involved with questions of economic development. In one of the most explicit efforts along these lines, Fukuyama argues that low-trust, highly communitarian societies are less likely to generate successful large enterprises than are high-trust societies, and low-trust societies typically have lower long-term rates of growth than do high trust ones.[19] Intriguingly, Fukuyama holds that capacities for direct, spontaneous or informal association of persons facilitate the establishment of large-scale, transparent and bureaucratic form of economic life, such as the large corporation. Rather than the two forms of association being mutually incompatible, the one is precondition for the other.

---

[12] Karl Polanyi, *The great transformation* (Boston: Beacon Press, 1957); Michael Polanyi, *The tacit dimension* (New York: Doubleday, 1966).

[13] Daniel Bell, *The cultural contradictions of capitalism* (New York: Basic Books, 1976).

[14] Robert D. Putnam, *Bowling alone: the collapse and revival of American community* (New York: Simon and Schuster, 2000); Michael J. Sandel, *Democracy's discontent: America in search of a public philosophy* (Cambridge, MA: Harvard/Belknap, 1996); Amitai Etzioni, *The new golden rule: community and morality in a democratic society* (New York: Basic Books, 1996); Levy, Tocqueville's revenge op. cit.; Robert N. Bellah *et al.*, *Habits of the heart: individualism and commitment in American life* (New York: Harper & Row, 1985).

[15] Putnam, Bowling alone op. cit.; James S. Coleman, *Foundations of social theory* (Cambridge: Harvard University Press, 1990).

[16] Michael Douglass and John Friedmann (eds.) *Cities for citizens* (Chichester: John Wiley & Sons., 1997).

[17] Anthony Giddens, *The consequences of modernity* (Stanford: Stanford University Press, 1990).

[18] Robert William Fogel, *The fourth Great Awakening and the future of egalitarianism* (Chicago: University of Chicago Press, 2000).

[19] Francis Fukuyama, *Trust: the social virtues and the creation of prosperity* (New York: Simon and Schuster, 1995).

Giddens and other sociologists extend the field of potential positive effects of community in the modern economy.[20] They start from a general point that contemporary modernization cannot be merely bureaucratic, whether Statist or corporate, because this tends to downplay individual autonomy and responsibility. He comes to the conclusion that in order to avoid the pitfalls of a rigid, administered society and economy, on the one hand, and a chaotic "jungle" on the other, intermediate levels of association are critical. Giddens and others specifically refer to communities as means to improve the functioning of labor markets, generate entrepreneurship, and organize the provision of the public goods which alleviate both private and state burdens in creating prosperity and social integration. Along these lines, success in small-firm based industrial clusters or districts, ranging from the most famous cases of Italy to examples drawn from Taiwan, Denmark, Mexico, or Germany, are also said to depend critically on the existence of communities which regulate complex inter-firm and firm-worker relationships through shared norms, reputation effects, and mutually-aligned expectations.[21] Most prominently, Putnam claims that "social capital" – which he defines specifically to mean levels of voluntary participation and civic engagement – is good for economic development and social integration.[22] Social capital creates positive externalities for the members of the societies that have high levels of it, so that even those who do not actively create it benefit from its existence. They concern such things as limiting moral hazards (e.g. less cheating in the economy, less crime in neighborhoods) and encouraging unpaid efforts (which then create benefits that spillover to others).

A closer look at Putnam's theoretical argument allows us to see some of its limits, but also how it may be adapted to a richer analysis of the institutional foundations of economic development. Putnam argues that there are two components of social capital: "bonding" among similar types of persons (class, ethnicity, background, interests) and "bridging" between different such groups or what he terms "people unlike ourselves." Bonding, in other words, operationalizes the classical notion of community, and bridging that of society. Moreover, Putnam argues that bonding is much easier to come by than bridging, and that where many different groups are present, it is much more difficult to achieve high levels of social capital than in more homogeneous societies. This suggests that bonding and bridging spring from different sources, and that they have complex relationships to one another.

---

[20] Giddens, The consequences of modernity *op. cit.*

[21] There is a vast literature on this subject. For extensive reviews, see, inter alia, Michael Storper, *The regional world: territorial development in a global economy* (New York: Guilford Press, 1997); Michael Storper and Robert Salais, *Worlds of production: the action frameworks of the economy* (Cambridge, MA: Harvard University Press, 1997); as well as the papers in Giacomo Becattini and Fabio Sforzi (eds.) *Lezioni sullo sviluppo locale* (Turin: Rosenberg & Sellier, 2002).

[22] Putnam, Bowling alone *op. cit.*

Putnam's concept of bonding bears obvious similarity to the standard notion of *Gemeinschaft*. In their study of the Third Italy, Putnam, Leonardi and Nanetti argue that social capital, embodied in group life of local, family networks and civic associationalism, emerges through long historical processes.[23] Actors trust each other because of their common cultural background, shared values, and strong reputation effects stem from dense interpersonal networks. This notion can also be found in many other empirical studies of regional economic development. [24]

Nonetheless, these definitions may be overly restrictive, because groups can exist in many other forms. Professional associations are based on shared norms of professional performance, not on shared history or interpersonal trust, for example. Along these lines, Aydogan has shown that even in the presence of shallow corporate cultures in Silicon Valley, due to a high level of labor turnover, professional culture makes possible a high level of industry- and region-specific social capital.[25] There is considerable bonding in Silicon Valley, but its networks of venture capitalists, technologists, and others have little to do with the trust- and tradition-based communities of the Third Italy. The bonds between members of a community can be modern as well as traditional, based on ascriptive or acquired traits, each activated through different signaling and screening mechanisms. It follows that communities should not be equated to the classical notion of mechanical solidarity or *Gemeinschaft*. In the same vein, the notions proposed by Fukuyama (trust), or the "civil society" theorists, may well be valid as empirical statements about the cases at hand, but they probably cannot be seen as general foundations of all community-type bonding. In addition, groups or communities do not necessarily express themselves as organizations or deliberate associations or Tocquevillian civic engagement.

Coleman attempted to deal with this issue by distinguishing "primordial" from organized social capital.[26] But he considered the former to be necessarily more powerful than the latter.[27] Primordial social bonding, in our view, should not be considered synonymous with ascriptive traits; there is no persuasive reason to believe that an acquired professional identity, for example[28], cannot be as primordial as, say, a regional or ethnic identity, with neither having to assume the form of organized civic associationalism or group membership. Moreover, as shall be argued below, the

---

[23] Robert D. Putnam, Robert Leonardi and Raffaella Y. Nanetti, *Making democracy work: civic traditions in modern Italy* (Princeton, NJ: Princeton University Press, 1993).

[24] Becattini and Sforzi, Lezioni sullo sviluppo locale *op. cit.*

[25] Nesli Aydogan, 'Social capital and growth in Silicon Valley' (Irvine, CA: UC Irvine, Department of Economics, Working Paper, 2002).

[26] Coleman, Foundations of social theory *op. cit.*

[27] Thanks to Arnaldo Bagnasco for calling my attention to this point (see Arnaldo Bagnasco, *Società fuora squadra* (Bologna: Il Mulino, 2003).

[28] The analytical basis for this argument can be found in section 2.1 below.

acquisition of such identities or memberships can be conceived as an expression of the individual's preferences and the exercise of rationality. Thus, though the sociological distinction between community and society is just as relevant as it ever was, many of the definitions of community are overly restrictive or arbitrary. "Community" will therefore be used here to refer to a wide range of reasons and ways of grouping together with others with whom we share some part of our identity, expectations, and interests. Social life is not just about the groups to which we belong, of course. Bridging is the core concern of all the social sciences interested in collective action and coordination: how can diverse agents reconcile their interests? In the presence of strong groups, how do such groups relate to each other? Can group interaction make something like "social choice" possible?

Much of the attention to groups, of course, has taken the form of studies of civic associationalism, and most students of associationalism have been concerned with issues of social integration rather than economics. However, there is longstanding concern with the role of voluntary association in social and economic development, of which Fukuyama and Putnam are the latest major entrants. Tocqueville thought that the Americans' capacity for association was one reason not only for their vibrant democracy, but also for the strength of American entrepreneurship.[29] Nonetheless, the literature is largely inconclusive about the relationship between associational life and economic development. For one thing, there are many cases of weakly associational societies that have done well as developers, including France, Singapore, the UK, Canada, and Australia. This is probably because associationalism can assume many different institutional forms, which determine its ultimate effects on economic development. Figure 1 illustrates some of the many possible combinations of these institutional forms, albeit in a highly schematic and simplified way. Some readers might quibble with the characterization of individual cases, but the illustration strongly suggests that there is no definite relationship between associationalism and developmental success or failure because there are so many different ways to bridge.

---

[29] Alexis de Tocqueville, *De la démocratie en Amérique* (1830) (Paris: Gallimard, 1986 edition, 2 volumes). The empirical indicator of these studies has always been the intensity of associational life, though there is considerable controversy over which empirical measures should be used and how to interpret them (Pippa Norris, *Democratic Phoenix: reinventing political activism* (Cambridge: Cambridge University Press, 2002)).

COMMUNITY: LEVELS OF CIVIC ASSOCIATION	SOCIETY: INSTITUTIONAL FORMS OF BRIDGING			
	Group-Oriented (groups are recognized as principal societal category in legal system, social policy)	Group-Oriented (groups are recognized as principal societal category in legal system, social policy)	Individualist (groups have secondary status in legal system, social policy, constitutional framework)	Individualist (groups have secondary status in legal system, social policy, constitutional framework)
	Non-comprehensive or decentralized group order: uneven corporatism or clannism	Comprehensive, centralized or organized group order: corporatism	Weak or incomplete liberalism and contractualism: tendency to distrust, fragile and limited circles	Strong and widespread liberalism and contractualism
Strongly associational	Third Italy Hong Kong Taiwan Jalisco, Mexico[30]	Japan Germany Denmark Sweden		USA Netherlands
Weakly associational or hierarchically associational	Italy Mezzogiorno Most of Mexico SE Brazil	France Singapore		United Kingdom Canada Australia New Zealand

Figure 1 Institutional forms and levels of civic association

This analysis echoes a broader point made forcefully by Granovetter and by Lin.[31] It is not just the density of ties that matters, but the structure of such bridges. The structure of ties is closely related to the mixture of power, compliance, sanctions, sharing, and cooperation on the part of the actors that are tied together. Thus, bonding and bridging should not be considered additive components of a single index of social capital, but rather independent and mutually shaping social forces.

---

[30] This is mentioned here specifically because it is one of the case studies that is reported on in other papers based on our fieldwork (see Lena Lavinas and Michael Storper, *Trajetórias para a economia do aprendizado: os novos mundos de produção no Nordeste* (Rio de Janeiro: research report to the Banco do Nordeste, prepared at IPEA, Rio, 1999)).

[31] Mark Granovetter, 'A theoretical agenda for economic sociology', in Mauro F. Guillén, Randall Collins, Paula England and Marshall Meyer (eds.) *The new economic sociology: developments in an emerging field* (New York: Russell Sage Foundation, 2002) pp. 35-60; Nan Lin, *Social capital: a theory of social structure and action* (New York: Cambridge University Press, 2001).

In this light, it can legitimately be asked whether there are certain kinds of bonds that are more suited to certain kinds of bridges, and vice-versa. If this were the case, there would be a kind of functionalist law of institutional structure and the forms of action it shapes. But most sociologists have long ago abandoned the idea of a single, unified social order, and few empirical students of institutions would subscribe to this notion today.[32] Rather than reflecting some kind of fixed functional compatibility ("certain kinds of communities are compatible with certain kinds of society," etc.), the relationship between society and community is better thought of as a dynamic and uncertain tension between bonds and bridges. The nature of this relationship and its effects on economic development is the principal concern of this paper.

2. Community, rationality and economy

Any nontrivial definition of community must define it as something more than the accidental and strictly temporary convergence of individual preferences. In the latter formulation, the analytical category of "group" or "community" is superfluous, because there is no aggregation of preferences exhibiting any significant degree of heterogeneity. To have some meaning, then, we must hold that communities or groups bring together individuals with at least some difference in preferences, who have the capacity for individual reflection about their preferences, and yet who are held together for collective action even in the face of some such differences and more than temporarily. This notion is largely rejected by contemporary analytic social science – economics, philosophy, political science – which display an extreme skepticism about any such putative social glue. In the dominant view, it is irrational for individuals to join groups because of the impossibility problem.[33] Groups can only sidetrack individuals from maximizing their preferences; the only kinds of preferences that matter are individual in nature; hence groups always diminish individual welfare and, to cap it all off, still cannot contribute to attaining an optimal level of overall preference satisfaction, i.e. they do not get us closer to "social choice".[34] If we believe that preference achievement is somehow related to economic effort and coordination, and if this powerful indictment of group life is well founded, then the existence of groups must be broadly bad for the process of economic

---

[32] Along these lines, see: Luc Boltanski and Laurent Thèvenot, *Les economies de la grandeur* (Paris: Gallimard, 1987); Anthony Giddens, *The constitution of society* (Cambridge: Polity Press, 1984); Neil Fligstein, *The architecture of markets: an economic sociology of twenty-first century capitalism and society* (Princeton, NJ: Princeton University Press, 2001); Sharon Zukin and Paul DiMaggio (eds.) *Structures of capital: the social organization of the economy* (New York: Cambridge University Press, 1990).

[33] Kenneth J. Arrow, *Social choice and individual values* (New York: Wiley, 1951).

[34] Buchanan and Tullock, The calculus of consent *op. cit.*

development.[35] It will not do, moreover, to argue that groups exist for various kinds of negative reasons, among which are the fear of sanctions (including reputation effects) for deviating from group norms, or because the costs of obtaining information or individually going out on one's own (i.e. transactions costs) are so high that one just gives up and lets oneself be carried along by the group. Real world groups may indeed exist for these reasons, but they are likely to suffer from the serious disadvantages predicted by theory.

These disadvantages are at the heart of contemporary institutional economics. The positive theory of institutions (PTI) provides solid microfoundations for the notion that communitarian forms of order often lead to rent-seeking, non-transparent behavior, and are prone to overwhelming principal-agent problems that frustrate the individual members of groups, while allowing small groups with passionately-held views to have undue influence over large less passionate majorities. These properties are then argued by economic historians and political economists to lead to sclerosis and lower levels of economic growth than can be had with clear dominance by societal (market) institutions.[36] This is a powerful critique of group life, and there is considerable empirical support for it. As a result, the PTI has been used to generate a dominant perspective that the only institutions we should have are those – such as property rights and the rule of law – which enforce the roles of competition and exit, and hence limit the role of bonding or communities.

2.1 Why are communities not necessarily all bad?

This is not the place to take on this vast and complex field of analytical philosophy and economics, but before going on to make some more direct observations about the potentially positive roles of communities in the market economy, it will be helpful to at least clear some of the analytical ground with respect to this extreme skepticism about group life. This can be done by summarizing the two principal objections to such skepticism which are detailed by Sen.[37]

In the first place, self-interest does not necessarily place actors in opposition to other actors in the way described by most theory. Freedom means the possibility to reasonably value something other than one's own monetary well-being; to be self-interested is not necessarily to be self-centered. It is reasonable for actors to pay attention to the demands of cooperation, and they are not only cooperative because of fear of sanctions (tit-for-tat reasons). According to Sen, the problem with rational

---

[35] Olson, The logic of collective action *op. cit.*

[36] Douglass North, *Structure and change in economic history* (New York: Norton, 1981); Olson, The logic of collective action *op. cit.*; Terry Moe, 'Interests, institutions and positive theory', *Studies in American Political Development* 2 (1987) pp. 236-99.

[37] Amartya Sen, *Rationality and freedom* (Cambridge: Harvard/Belknap, 2002).

choice theory in this regard is that it rejects any possible rival understandings of what might lie behind the regularity of choices, and notably that choices that are not narrowly self-interested can be reasonably judged to be rational for the individual.[38] Moreover, the unit of agency in choice can itself be broader than individual action: self-goal choice is not the only kind of choice. All of this leads to a view where what is to be maximized may well incorporate broader consequences, such as group actions and processes, and where this broadened maximand can be considered an "*as if* objective function"[39]. In these cases, individuals may have preferences over comprehensive outcomes (and not just discrete or "culmination" outcomes).[40]

But can such preference-defined groups contribute to a broader achievement of coordination in society, i.e. lead us in the direction of "social choice?" It is conceivable that even if the existence of some groups can be defended as stemming from rational choices, they simply partake of the impossibility problem. The formal precondition for the impossibility of social choice to disappear is that there exist information that would make possible interpersonal comparisons of social welfare judgements and that even partial comparisons can be helpful.[41] Here, groups may be useful in two ways. We mentioned above that true – non second-best – groups do not exist *merely* because information on alternatives is costly;[42] but if groups make it possible for individuals better to compare preferences, for whatever reason, including lowering the costs of good information or judgements, then they do assist in achieving the possibility of social choice. In this sense, as Sen points out, "choice problems come in many shapes and sizes," and groups can help expand the shapes and sizes that actually get considered, both substantively and procedurally.

Finally, social choice theory has always based its impossibility judgements on reasoning which does not take account of distributional questions (leading to Pareto efficiency criteria). But if, as we shall suggest in later sections, groups are key to achieving satisfactory distributional arrangements in the economy which in turn contribute to higher rates of economic development, then it follows that the refusal to consider distributional issues is misplaced.

Economics has done very well in the "sophisticated analysis of how individuals pursue incentives in well-defined social spaces."[43]. The problem is, of course, that more complex institutional contexts of individual and social choice drop out of that picture. Having now remarked why this might be true in a rather abstract analytical

---

[38] Sen, Rationality and freedom *op. cit.*, p. 28.
[39] Ibid., p. 41.
[40] Ibid., p. 45.
[41] Ibid., p. 96.
[42] Or if individuals are too lazy to investigate alternatives.
[43] Granovetter, 'A theoretical agenda for economic sociology' *op. cit.*

sense, we can now move on to some of the more real world ways in which groups can make positive necessary contributions to economic development.

2.2 Successful markets require communities

These contributions of society and community come about because they minimize moral hazards, reduce transactions costs and generate certain kinds of positive externalities and increasing returns effects. Some of the founding figures of modern economics – such as Alfred Marshall – intimated that community was sometimes indispensable to superior economic performance.[44] Marshall's writings about the textile districts of Lancashire, which he so admired, are shot through with ambivalence. In some passages, he describes them as fully competitive systems; in others, he observes that "the secrets of industry are in the air," i.e. collective resources of the community of producers. Twentieth century economists, however, progressively came along to the view that perfect markets depend on the existence of *Gesellschaft*, seeing *Gemeinschaft* as a barrier to their full realization for the reasons adumbrated above.

It does not follow theoretically or empirically, however, that the economy would be better off entirely without communities. One can certainly question the veracity of this skepticism about communities on empirical grounds alone. As we have already noted, the continuing tendency to define groups or communities using the 19th century sociological distinction is an ongoing source of confusion. Margaret Thatcher attracted attention by her provocative declaration that "society doesn't exist, only individuals exist." From a social science standpoint, of course, she mangled the standard notion i.e. that it is society (*Gesellschaft*) which is precisely an aggregation of individuals organized according to transparent, modern principles; she probably meant to criticize communities as the source of hide-bound tradition and corporatism. Nonetheless, economics is also at fault when it sees all traditional, primordial groups as anti-competitive and rent-seeking; there is a huge case study literature on economic networks which shows the contrary.[45] Moreover, as noted previously, groups or communities are not necessarily held together through tradition, interpersonal relations, and non-rational bonds between people. This is indeed sometimes the case, but other examples, such as that of Silicon Valley, suggest a different point of view.

---

[44] Alfred Marshall, *Industry and trade* (London: Macmillan, 1919).

[45] E.g. Gernot Grabher (ed.) *The embedded firm: on the socioeconomics of industrial networks* (London: Routledge, 1993); Edward H. Lorenz, 'Neither friends nor strangers: informal networks of subcontracting in French industry', in Gambetta, Trust *op. cit.*, pp. 194-210; Lin, Social capital *op. cit.*

The response to this mainstream view of institutions creating excessive transactions costs, moral hazards, and rent-seeking is not only empirical, however. Transactions costs economics, as developed by Williamson[46] and others, points to the necessary emergence of certain kinds of non-market based coordination; for example, under some circumstances, relational contracting is more efficient than spot markets in perfect competition. The efficiency of such contracting is enhanced by interfirm networks of actors. Nonetheless, in economics there remains a great deal of ambiguity about this point. Much of the "new institutional economics" strains to find the perfectly rational character of participation in networks and governance, denying that these could be – at least partially – dependent on group membership or that the participants could be socially "embedded" in ways important to the functioning of these groups. Many students of such networks hold that relations are not enforced merely by the threat of sanctions, but by some kind of bonding, whether primordial or acquired.[47] These may be combined with the "societal" pressures of sanctions, but even sanctions may be more efficient in the presence of communitarian bonds.

The new economics of information offers a second, more fundamental challenge within economics to the society-only view of economic coordination. It shows that information-based market failures are general to modern capitalism, and other kinds of organization than markets must fill in the breach. Greenwald and Stiglitz note that when information is not complete, and it is almost never complete, markets are incomplete.[48] The resulting market failures are not the same as the classical market failures of welfare economics, because the new ones are pervasive and difficult to identify and isolate. In turn, Stiglitz suggests that communities are one of the ways that these market failures can be efficiently overcome, and that they are often superior to bureaucracies.[49] No precise definition of community is given, but it is clearly intimated that groups have a necessary role in achieving optimal coordination of a well-functioning modern economy.

This critique takes on both the positive theory of institutions and transactions costs economics on their own grounds, for it suggests that there is no way for markets always to be the route to optimal reduction of transactions costs, moral hazards, and other incentive problems. In other words, it gives theoretical support to

---

[46] Oliver E. Williamson, *The economic institutions of capitalism: markets, firms, relational contracting* (New York: Free Press, 1985).

[47] Edward H. Lorenz, 'Trust, community, and cooperation: toward a theory of industrial districts', in Michael Storper and Allen J. Scott (eds.) *Pathways to industrialization and regional development* (London: Routledge, 1992) pp. 195-204.

[48] Bruce Greenwald, Joseph E. Stiglitz and Andrew Weiss, 'Informational imperfections in the capital market and macroeconomic fluctuations', *American Economic Review* 74, 2 (1984) pp. 194-99; Bruce Greenwald and Joseph E. Stiglitz, 'Externalities in economies with imperfect information and incomplete markets', *Quarterly Journal of Economics* 101 (1986) pp. 229-64.

[49] Joseph E. Stiglitz, *Whither socialism?* (Cambridge, MA: MIT Press, 1994).

the notion which emerges from much empirical work, i.e. that communities are actually quite good, under some circumstances, at all these tasks.

But this is not all. Contemporary growth theory has shown that accumulation of human capital is the central element in growth, and that there is tight complementarity between human capital and technology. Lucas (1988) argues that human capital accumulates when the rate of return to additional increments of human capital is higher than the discount rate.[50] This rate of return is defined via a social process and is not just the outcome of individual education or effort. The reason, of course, is that the degree to which acquired knowledge can actually be applied in the economy depends on other people: it can rarely be done alone. Sometimes, the application of human or technological capital requires the bond of "matching" with those who have similiar skills or capital, i.e. where scale effects are necessary. Sometimes it requires linking up with those who have complementary skills or technologies, without which our capital cannot be used in isolation. Knowledgeable (skilled) agents tend therefore to function via selective affinities, within selected economic communities. If these affinities do not exist at all (i.e. knowledgeable people are either extremely rare so they can match up with nobody, or they are extremely distrustful), knowledge will be wasted, and have little positive developmental effect. When collective action of this type is realized, moreover, knowledge spillovers are activated and there are increasing returns to knowledge investments.[51] This is why so many empirical studies have shown that intra-group solidarity facilitates acquisition of human capital and deployment of new technologies, and inter-group conflicts and rivalries slow down or even impede growth from occurring.[52]

All in all then, there are secure reasons to believe that communities – as we have defined them – are essential underpinnings of the incentives to economic effort. They are not replacements for individual incentives. Moreover, as we shall now observe, the possible positive contributions of bonding are maximized, and its possible negative effects minimized, when it is married to appropriate societal forces, i.e. bridging processes.

---

[50] Robert E. Lucas, 'The mechanics of economic development', *Journal of Monetary Economics* 22 (1988) pp. 3-42.

[51] William Easterly, *The elusive quest for growth: economists' adventures and misadventures in the tropics* (Cambridge, MA: MIT Press, 2001).

[52] Alice H. Amsden, *The rise of the "rest:" challenges to the West from late-industrializing economies.* (Oxford: Oxford University Press, 2001); Easterly, The elusive quest for growth *op. cit.*

3. Bridging: The politics of development

As noted, much economics claims that sclerosis is the almost-inevitable outcome of institutionalization of inter-group relations. But even such theory does not deny that there are better and worse ways to weave particular groups together. Much recent research on economic development has demonstrated that political coalition formation is essential to the process. The principal explanations supplied for why coalitions are so important are that they provide a context in which good ideas and policies can be implemented; they allow problem-solving and conflict resolution. Much recent analytical effort has gone into theorizing how much democratic political competition, institutional checks and balances, or administrative isolation are necessary to counteract the tendency for special interest politics to extract rents and drag down efficiency, the latter being the favorite theme of classics in political economy such as Schattschneider, Buchanan and Tullock, and Olson.[53]

As we shall now see, however, almost all of the research on coalitions is about intergroup relations, with relatively little attention given to underlying social forces, especially bonding, and hence to the possible interaction of bonding and bridging in encouraging coalition formation and in shaping the ways that coalitions actually function. Two main versions of this argument shall now be examined.

3.1 Democracy as a developmental community

Development economists have long speculated on a possible relationship between the long-term potential for economic development and the existence of democratic institutions, where democracy is, in the terms of the present argument, a form of society. Democracy permits the market system to function correctly, in this view, because democratic institutions presuppose the individual rights that underlie factor mobility and individual initiative, while democratic political processes encourage inter-group competition that both holds rent-earning behavior in check and encourages compromise and moderation. [54]

In the recent context of globalization, this argument has been refocused around the relationship between integration, democracy and development.[55] One such theory is an extension of the classical *doux commerce* thesis.[56] Most cases of backwardness are

---

[53] E.E. Schattschneider, *Politics, pressures and the tariff* (Englewood Cliffs, NJ: Prentice Hall, 1935); Buchanan and Tullock, The calculus of consent *op. cit.*; Olson, The logic of collective action *op. cit.*

[54] Seymour Martin Lipset, *Political man* (Garden City, NY: Doubleday Anchor, 1963).

[55] Whether of less-developed regions into their respective national economies or integration of national economies with different levels of development – as in the EU or NAFTA, or integration generally into the world economy.

[56] Albert Hirschman, *The passions and the interests* (Princeton, NJ: Princeton University Press, 1997).

attributed to an excess of community – clannism, rigidity, and closure – and a deficiency of societal structures capable of creating efficient markets to offset or defeat these communitarian forces. Trade brings about economic interdependency, which forces places to develop institutional configurations that support such integration, in the form of markets and a commitment to transparency and property rights. This in turn necessitates certain kinds of democratic institutions, because they are the only ones truly compatible with high degrees of factor mobility, competition (instead of rent-seeking), and entrepreneurship. Commerce thus brings these latter into existence and eliminates the excesses of community.

However, all of these arguments do rather poorly in empirical terms. Thus, Przeworski et al.,[57] in the most extensive statistical analysis of the relationship between democracy and development to date, show that there is nothing that can show whether democracy is the outcome of development or its precursor; there are also many examples of spectacular reversals of democracies in the face of rapidly rising trade, and of booms during authoritarian periods.

Another contemporary argument reverses the causality of the *doux commerce* thesis. Rodrik shows that there are strong relationships between the ability of a society to manage distributional conflicts when faced with shocks to the economy,[58] and hence its ability to implement policies capable of maintaining growth. Shocks bring out latent conflicts and present strong dangers that wrong policies will be adopted, reflecting merely the interests of the most powerful (rent-seeking) agents, and this will generate ongoing conflict. The successful resolution of such potential conflicts, goes the argument, is strongly linked to the existence of democratic institutions and processes, because these provide a forum for expression and consensus-building, or at least for cooperation and acceptance of sacrifice in the name of the commonwealth. It is held that formal democracy depends on clear and transparent social interaction, very similar in form and flavor to the kinds of transactions that underpin a market economy, even if the rights and constituencies associated with each are different. Thus, the culture that underpins these two kinds of processes is a common and mutually reinforcing one, with democracy necessary to reap the full benefits of commerce.

Even if the latter argument is still somewhat simplistic in its definition of the qualities of "democracy," it does better empirically than the standard version of the *doux commerce* thesis. As Rodrik notes, the "voluminous empirical literature on the long-run consequences of political democracy for economic growth has generally

---

[57] Adam Przeworski, Michael Alvarez, José Antonio Cheibub and Fernando Limongi, *Democracy and development: political institutions and well-being in the world, 1950-1990* (Cambridge: Cambridge University Press, 2000).

[58] Dani Rodrik, *The new global economy and developing countries: making openness work* (Washington, DC: Overseas Development Council, 1999).

yielded ambiguous results ... however, more recent studies show that democracies produce a better balance between risk and reward: that is, the level of aggregate economic instability tends to be much lower under democracies."[59] Hence, economies in formally democratic countries perform systematically better when confronted with external shocks, and have higher long-term growth rates.

There is further, albeit indirect, empirical support for this point of view. Below a certain income level, some forms of dictatorship may do as well as democracy because they can centralize power and thereby control corruption and rent-seeking. Democracies, however, never fall once a certain level of development has been achieved (the threshold is set at US$6055 per capita today).[60] This appears to be the case because wealthier democracies and dictatorships grow differently: the former are more technology-intensive and less labor intensive in the way national wealth is increased. Ultimately, this translates into higher wages in democracies, because people respond by lowering fertility, which they also do because the rule of law typical of wealthy democracies makes them more confident in a predictable future, less dependent on arbitrary power.[61] This also explains why there are no authoritarian regimes at extremely high income levels. It is thus a short extension of this to the notion that wealthy, internally heterogeneous democracies are more flexible and efficacious at solving problems in a way which is compatible with long-term economic efficiency.

However, the arguments of both Rodrik and the standard *doux commerce* notion are fundamentally unclear about whether democratic processes succeed due to societal rules or to social forces which amount to a democratic community. One of the reasons the detailed empirical results of Przeworski *et al.* are inconclusive is that they define democracy rather narrowly as formal electoral and legislative procedures.[62] Lindert shows that the democracy-growth connection is very strong when democracy is defined more broadly as the substantive existence of "voice" in the economy, including not just big electoral institutions, but many small practices that organize and allow participation and political-economic competition.[63] Lindert calls attention to the specific role of educational institutions in determining who has voice, but the general point is about the "wider distribution of voice"[64], which we have argued is in many respects indelibly communitarian.

---

[59] Ibid., p. 101.

[60] Przeworski *et al.*, Democracy and development *op. cit.*

[61] Alberto Alesina, Sule Ozler, Nouriel Roubini and Phillip Swagel, 'Political instability and economic growth', *Journal of Economic Growth* 1 (1996): 189-212.

[62] Przeworski *et al.*, Democracy and development *op. cit.*

[63] Peter H. Lindert, 'Voice and growth: was Churchill right?' (Cambridge, MA: NBER Working Paper No. w9749, June 2003) *www.nber.org/papers/w9749*.

[64] Ibid., p. 30.

This does not imply that democracy is unrelated to formal bridging, i.e. the opportunity to sustain formal political coalitions between groups. There is abundant evidence that religious, ethnic and regional fragmentation are strongly associated with more frequent regime change for both authoritarian and democratic regimes, and with a propensity to authoritarianism. Negotiating the bridges generally occurs when democratic principles are widely accepted, and the resulting democracies are longer-lasting and more stable than authoritarian or corporatist marriages of different groups, with better effects on long-term growth.[65]

In this light, it seems likely that the existence and survival of democratic institutions is due to both bonding and bridging. Appealing to the mere existence of formally democratic institutions in more developed economies largely begs the question of how – politically – a society's communities are brought into an economically successful relationship with each other. Even if commerce has a role in this process, it is certainly not anything like the automatic "calling forth" of the institutions and social practices, cited above, which are functionally necessary to markets. Indeed, much of the causality must run the other way around, with patterns of bonding and bridging likely to determine the capacity of specific institutions for solving economic problems, which in turn enhances economic development.

3.2 Developmental coalitions as bridges between communities

Political scientists and sociologists who are more interested in the classical questions of politics and interests, rather than the micro-foundations of institutions, have tried to identify the politics of successful developmental coalitions and the institutional forms of successful developmental states. Public choice theory does not share this interest in coalitions and states, holding instead that aggregation of interests can and should be generated spontaneously and temporarily. In this view, both who bonds and how they bridge with other groups emerge from rational action under a condition of full information transparency and low to nil transactions costs. Such "Coasian" bargains assume away precisely the conditions which, we have argued in section 2.2, are defining features of the modern economy and which create necessary and efficiency-enhancing roles for groups. More promising, in our view, political economists observe that certain political opportunity structures allow for creation of developmentally-effective political coalitions and the containment of rent-seeking, non-competitive behavior. Sociologists deal with this issue by emphasizing relations between institutions (especially States) and their societies, in determining whether states have the societal support to organize good development strategies.

---

[65] Easterly, The elusive quest for growth *op. cit.*; Przeworski *et al.*, Democracy and development *op. cit.*

Along these lines, a wide body of detailed, close-to-the-ground research has shown that the long-term upward spirals of the East Asian, Irish, Israeli (until recently) and even Mauritian economies – to name just a few – have been made possible by intelligent developmental strategies.[66] These strategies have been implemented by well-trained and honest bureaucrats[67] with significant long-term public sector policy involvement; they depend on successful regulation of capital markets and channeling of foreign investment; and they rely on institutionally-nurtured long-term entrepreneurship as a principal source of efficiency and competitiveness.

The question then is: Why have these places been able to develop the institutional wherewithal to succeed, aside from large doses of good timing, good luck, and good training of their bureaucrats? The economic practices favorable to development[68] emerge when they can be made to prevail in domestic politics, through formation of coalitions which back these practices.[69] Where do such coalitions come from? One response is to claim that success has come from the establishment of political coalitions whose interests, fortuitously, corresponded to "good economics," while less successful places are dominated by coalitions whose interests correspond to bad economics.[70] However, even Haggard admits that all such coalitions cannot simply be based on a fortuitous coalescence of the interests of each member. This is because they involve distributional tradeoffs, and short-term sacrifices from certain members.

This modifies the question, from searching for perfect convergence of interests, to asking how such coalitions can emerge on the basis of short- to medium-term sacrifices of interests, and development of a common vision of common potential long-term interests. Haggard claims that, in part, the insulation of political elites from certain kinds of interest-based pressures allows them to formulate policies with high long-run payoffs. There is substantial mediation of political choices by institutions and ideas, not just by interests (or at least that ideas transform the time horizons used in defining interests).

---

[66] Robert Wade, *Governing the market: economic theory and the role of government in East Asian industrialization* (Princeton, NJ: Princeton University Press, 1990); Peter Evans, *Embedded autonomy: states and industrial transformation* (Princeton: Princeton University Press, 1995); Alice H. Amsden, *Asia's next giant: South Korea and late industrialization* (Oxford: Oxford University Press, 1992); Amsden, The rise of the "rest" *op. cit.*; Eoin O'Malley, 'Industrial policy in Ireland and the problem of late development', in Michael Storper, Stavros B. Thomadakis and Lena J. Tsipouri (eds.) *Latecomers in the global economy* (London: Routledge, 1998) pp. 203-23.

[67] The New Comparative Economics emphasize, in this regard, the very long run of "law and order" and the "rule of law," defined respectively the extent to which a rule-bound state is in place, and the extent to which actors are obliged to follow the rules that are established (Andrei Shleifer, 'The new comparative economics', *NBER Reporter* (Fall 2002) pp. 12-15).

[68] Amsden, The rise of the "rest" *op. cit.* calls them "control systems," consisting of good mutual obligations and the respect of these obligations.

[69] Ibid.; Evans, Embedded autonomy *op. cit.*

[70] Stephan Haggard, *Pathways from the periphery* (Ithaca, NY: Cornell University Press, 1990).

If this were the case, however, then successful development would simply require the right political opportunity structures, i.e. appropriate formal institutions that respect the independence of technocrats.[71] The two principal doubts about this argument are, on the one hand, that countries with similar political opportunity structures do very differently with their experts; in some, isolation seems to manifest itself, while in others it does not. On the other hand, isolation does not lead to universally intelligent economic decisionmaking, any more than does total immersion in the rough and tumble of society.[72] For these questions, no purely institutional explanation of public policy will do: some deeper set of forces affects the actual functioning degree of isolation of decisions and their intelligence. In this vein, Aghion *et al.* argue that the degree of underlying social polarization or fragmentation[73] is positively associated with the insulation of decision-making from day to-day-politics.[74] Hence, potentially conflictual societies "choose" insulation, while more unified ones choose more "democratic" systems. Yet this view has a difficult time accounting for the high level of insulation in Japan and Korea (relatively homogeneous societies), the low level in the USA (another homogeneous country according to their definition), and the evident fact that developmental success can be had in low insulation political structures like those of the USA or Canada, as well as in high insulation situations such as Korea or Japan.

Still, many authors confirm that primordial bonding patterns set the basic parameters for the problem of societal bridging. These include the degree of racial,

---

[71] See, for contrasting positions, Amsden, The rise of the "rest" *op. cit.* and Gene M. Grossman and Elhanan Helpman, *Special interest politics* (Cambridge, MA: MIT Press, 2001).

[72] Along these lines, the coalitions brought into being by such political opportunity structures must in any case have means of surviving. One could argue, simply, that they either survive in the successful cases because of their success with development, while in the other cases, they survive by providing rents to the powerful. But all development processes generate ongoing potential for conflict, and require internal adjustments. Are these adjustments achievable simply through the inertia of political opportunity structures (intelligent insulated elites in the successful cases, or powerful rent-seeking coalitions in the others)? This seems more plausible for developmental blockage than success. Successful coalitions must ultimately be good at resolving the real conflicts engendered by development, by drawing on the real communities of interest in existence and maintaining them in some viable societal relationship to one another. In other words, successful political coalitions depend for their formation not only on fortuitous institutional set-ups and good ideas; they also respond to ongoing interactions of communities which make up the society in question. This brings us full circle to the existence of law and order and the rule of law, but these do not exist as abstract societal forces; they exist as concrete practices that different communities use to bridge their interactions with other communities.

[73] Philippe Aghion, Alberto Alesina and Francesco Trebbi, 'Endogenous political institutions' (Cambridge, MA: NBER Working Paper w9006, June 2002) *www.nber.org/papers/w9006*. The sources of such fragmentation might be ethnic, regional or class-based.

[74] But this relationship weakens as countries become richer, because the need for large reforms becomes smaller and losses can be compensated at costs which represent small proportions of total societal wealth. Hence, there is a generally lower need for political insulation.

ethnic, language, economic, and geographical homogeneity or diversity of the society in question. Easterly shows that the more ethnic or racial divisions there are in a society, the more tendency there is for rent-seeking behavior to undermine developmentalist policy and efficient use of foreign aid.[75] Amsden holds that societies with less income inequality have done better in implementing strategies for becoming major manufacturing powers.[76] This is because equality between individuals cuts across groups and makes it more difficult to disenfranchise other groups and/or subject them to rent-earning behavior by the dominant groups. It also, as Aghion points out,[77] eliminates the disincentive to effort that extreme inequality can generate, a point echoed by Amartya Sen.[78] Racial and ethnic homogeneity often, but not always, correspond to lower levels of income inequality and hence reinforce each other in promoting bridging, which in turn helps to achieve consensus around developmental objectives. Amsden claims specifically that such consensus manifests itself in the capacity to establish "control systems," consisting of enforceable mutual obligations between states and firms.[79] Alesina and Rodrik argue that lower inequality reduces the need for redistributive politics which sap growth-producing investment.[80] In another vein, sociologists such as Pizzorno[81] emphasized that becoming a "middle class" society was both a result of the acquiring of common values – echoing the point made in the previous section about democracy as a form of community – and because the habits of the middle class are bridges between people with different primordial bonds, a set of practices they share, a common language.[82]

Nonetheless, the contemporary field of political economy shows that there can be no direct passage from these underlying parameters of diversity and equality to developmental outcomes, as is suggested by Figure 2.

---

[75] Easterly, The elusive quest for growth *op. cit.*

[76] Amsden, The rise of the "rest" *op. cit.*

[77] Philippe Aghion, 'Inequality and economic growth', in Philippe Aghion and Jeffrey G. Williamson, *Growth, inequality and globalization* (Cambridge: Cambridge University Press, 1998) pp. 5-102.

[78] Amartya Sen, *Development as freedom* (New York: Knopf, 1999).

[79] Amsden, The rise of the "rest" *op. cit.*

[80] Alberto Alesina and Dani Rodrik, 'Distributive politics and economic growth', *Quarterly Journal of Economics* 109 (1994) pp. 465-90.

[81] Alessandro Pizzorno, *I soggetti del pluralismo: classi, partiti, sindicati* (Bologna: Il Mulino, 1980).

[82] This also echoes Lipset's notion of cross-cutting diversified alliances as generating a kind of moderation, generalized bridging; Lipset, Political man *op. cit.*

	HIGH EQUALITY	HIGH INEQUALITY
HETEROGENEITY/ DIVERSITY	<ul><li>corporatist democracy?</li><li>paralyzed corporatism?</li><li>beneficial political competition?</li><li>special interest paralysis?</li></ul>	<ul><li>authoritarian plundering elite?</li><li>insider/outsider developmental regime?</li></ul>
HOMOGENEITY	<ul><li>developmentalist dictatorship?</li><li>Scandinavian democracy?</li><li>hierarchical, Asian-style obligational system</li></ul>	<ul><li>plundering elite?</li><li>developmental elite?</li></ul>

Figure 2 Societal unity and development regimes

Political economists point out that there are political opportunity structures in between these structural features of the society and the type of regime which is established. But then we are simply back to the issue raised by Aghion and the school of comparative economics, i.e. how underlying configurations of social forces give rise to institutions, i.e. political opportunity structures and economic governance regimes.

To get around this risk of infinite regress in the analysis, then, the question must be reframed, in three ways. One is to lower the level of aggregation or abstraction, and to analyze bonding and bridging in relationship to specific domains of economic problem-solving. The relevant institutions are not just constitutions, legal regimes, and political-electoral systems, nor even just formal institutions that regulate labor and capital markets, but also include a wide range of quotidian ways that groups create voice and how they relate to each other, much in the same way that was suggested for the democracy question in section 3.1.[83] Another is to see bonding and bridging as interactive, mutually transformative processes, rather than determined by fixed functional parameters, at one extreme, or totally malleable according to Coasian bargains, at the other extreme. A third is to hold that bonding and bridging have causes which are, at least partially, independent of formal institutional architecture and political opportunity structures, that they drive the different economic performances of institutions and governance regimes and they also affect the "choice" of such regimes.

---

[83] Along the lines of this focus on "small" and not just big institutions, we can cite economic historians like O'Rourke and Williamson who claim that the "Industrial Revolution" was not a revolution, but a long drawn-out process of rising productivity through many small improvements, and good incremental problem-solving. Technological breakthroughs helped, but in order to have their full effect, they required wide, long, and deep ongoing institutional complements. Kevin H. O'Rourke and Jeffrey G. Williamson, 'From Malthus to Ohlin: trade, growth and distribution since 1500' (Cambridge, MA: NBER Working Paper No. w8955, May 2002) www.nber.org/papers/w8955.

4. How society and community frame incentives

As we have seen, markets and development pathways require both bonding and bridging. In markets, transactions costs and moral hazards may be reduced by communities and by societal rules and practices. Spillovers which are at the heart of achieving the increasing returns which are central to the growth process can only be achieved in the presence of certain kinds of bonds between people, but rigid bonds or too much social hierarchy may also inhibit them from coming about. Developmental pathways require bridging between people, without which the coalitions that make it possible to deal with problems and governance are impossible, but bridging is ultimately strongly shaped by the underlying patterns of bonding or communities.

Communitarian and societal forces interact, necessarily, in shaping the complex institutional contexts that actors face. What do they do when they interact? They shape the basic ways that individuals can participate in the economy, creating incentives for them to do some things and not do others. This is why considering society and community in interaction allows us to analyze the formation of incentives under institutional conditions which are *not* "well controlled." Society and community are in a sort of delicate interaction with each other, generating a wide variety of strengths and weaknesses in the development process, and doing so differently across space and time.

What are these incentives? The first column of Figure 3 lists three main institutional areas in which certain first-order conditions for economic growth must be satisfied: those that assure microeconomic efficiency; those that define social policy underpinnings of such efficiency; and those that encourage effective problem-solving.[84]

To take the first such feature, any set of forces which systematically reduces transactions costs and moral hazards creates a microeconomic environment that comes across to individual actors as the possibility to have confidence in the economic process and to better estimate future rewards. This environment is reflected in discount rates, risk perceptions[85] and the estimation of long-term wealth accumulation prospects, leading to higher expectations and effort levels. These in turn have many beneficial effects on long-term economic performance by encouraging actors to participate in the routines that are favorable to the economy, which are shown in column three. They include encouraging innovative (Schumpeterian) entrepreneur-

---

[84] See also Dani Rodrik, 'Growth strategies' (Cambridge, MA: NBER Working Paper No. w10050, October 2003) *www.nber.org/papers/w10050*. There is of course a fourth area, macroeconomics, but that is beyond the scope of the present paper.

[85] We are reminded here of the fundamental distinction between risk and uncertainty, introduced by Frank Knight in his *Risk, uncertainty and profit* (New York: AH Kelly, 1921). When confidence is weak or absent, the problem is that risks can no longer be estimated and hence minimized, and actors must face true uncertainty, with strongly negative effects on many of the foundations of long-term growth.

ship[86]; improving the coordination of inter-firm transactions, both lowering costs and raising the willingness of firms to try to construct them, hence improving the growth-inducing effects of the economy-wide division of labor;[87] and raising investment levels through the abovementioned effects on discount rates and risk perceptions.

Confidence is directly related to the central mechanism of contemporary growth theory, which is the accumulation and application of knowledge.[88] As noted earlier, knowledge is different from many other factors of production, in that it can have increasing returns because it can be re-used at no additional cost and can be applied in many different ways and recombined into different uses; these features permit it to avoid diminishing returns. Communities facilitate the selective affinities underlying knowledge spillovers and snowball effects in its application. At the same time, if knowledge stays too much inside such communities – when communities mistrust each other – then development will have a limited and uneven spread; so, there need to be ways of bridging between communities, in other words ways of providing more knowledgeable communities with confidence that their knowledge will be well used by members of other communities. Mutual confidence through both bonding and bridging is essential, then, to creating knowledge-based growth. In addition, confidence encourages governments to be less myopic in their policies, and myopic governmental policies have been shown to be harmful to growth.[89]

The second feature is an effective social policy environment, as reflected in distributional arrangements – not to be confused with the absence of distributional conflict. When there are social forces that generate acceptable distributional arrangements, such arrangements will encourage necessary sacrifices to be made when economies undergo the inevitable shocks and setbacks of any development process.[90] Thus, it also has a positive incentive effect. Aghion has argued that excessive inequality is just as bad as excessive income levelling, because too much inequality simply leads to withdrawal of effort by potentially productive actors; formally, it amounts to a capital market imperfection.[91]

---

[86] Mark Casson, *Entrepreneurship and business culture* (Aldershot, Hants, UK: Edward Elgar, 1995); Israel Kirzner, *Competition and entrepreneurship* (Chicago: University of Chicago Press, 1973); Schumpeter, Joseph A., *The economics and sociology of capitalism*, edited by Richard Swedberg (Princeton, NJ: Princeton University Press, 1991).

[87] Allyn Young, 'Increasing returns and economic progress', *Economic Journal* 38 (1928) pp. 527-42; George J. Stigler, 'The division of labor is limited by the extent of the market', *Journal of Political Economy* 69 (1951) pp. 213-25.

[88] Lucas, 'The mechanics of economic development' *op. cit.*

[89] Torsten Persson and Guido Tabellini, *Political economics: explaining economic policy* (Cambridge, MA: MIT Press, 2002).

[90] Rodrik, The new global economy and developing countries *op. cit.*

[91] Aghion, 'Inequality and economic growth' *op. cit.* These have an indirect link to Sen's notion that extreme inequality expresses the lack of, but also impedes the construction of, the social bonds

INCENTIVES NECESSARY TO LONG-TERM DEVELOPMENT	PRINCIPAL MICRO-ECONOMIC EFFECTS OF EACH INCENTIVE	OPERATIONAL INSTITUTIONS: BEHAVIOR, ROUTINES, REGULARITIES
MICROECONOMIC: Generate confidence ↓	▪ Reduces transactions costs (coordination) ▪ Reduces moral hazards (incentives) ▪ Raises expectations and efforts: discount rate (incentives) ↓	▪ Encourages Schumpeterian entrepreneurship ▪ Improves coordination of firm-firm transactions ▪ Raises investment levels ↓
SOCIAL POLICY: Effective and acceptable distributional arrangements ↓↓	▪ precedent encourages ongoing 'sacrifices' in face of shocks (incentives) ▪ Overcomes disincentive to participate and make effort: limits to exploitative rent-seeking (incentives) ▪ Overcomes disincentive to invest and create employment: limits to revanchist rent-seeking (incentives) ▪ Improves willingness to pay taxes (incentives) ↓↓	▪ Raises investments in skills ▪ Raises work and entrepreneurial participation rates ▪ Raises public investment levels, some of which lower business costs ↓↓
PROBLEM-SOLVING: Adjustments of incentives and coordination, prevent sclerosis	▪ Participation of groups enhanced (incentives, coordination) ▪ minimize rent-seeking from corporatism (incentives, coordination)	▪ Better adjustment of rules governing entrepreneurship and labor markets ▪ Intelligent ideas more likely to receive support as public policy ▪ Coalitions can form, avoiding chaotic instability

Figure 3 The foundations of development

In the context of knowledge matching and spillover effects, appropriate distributional arrangements encourage participation and discourage withdrawal of effort – whether between or within groups. One way in which they do this is by providing incentives for those who are not the greatest beneficiaries of new

---

which are crucial to development, because it discourages provision of certain necessary social goods and deprives the poorest of the preconditions (basic resources) which would enable them to contribute to their own, and society's, development; Sen, *Development as freedom op. cit.*

technologies to support (or at least not block) innovations, generally most strongly pushed by those who stand to benefit the most from them.[92] There is a balance to be achieved between individual and group incentives in order to minimize moral hazards but maximize complementarity effects. Alesina and Rodrik and Persson and Tabellini argue theoretically that less inequality has a positive relationship to growth,[93] which is consistent with the empirical evidence which shows that the Highly Performing Asian Economies (HPAEs) have all been characterized by limited inequality, in contrast to the poorly-performing Latin American economies. Moderation in inequality improves overall investments in skill creation, raises the incentives to participate fully in the formal economy and to become an entrepreneur (hence, participation rates and levels), and improves the willingness to pay taxes and to invest. Effective distributional arrangements are central to achieving the spillovers we identified in section 2.2 as essential to long-term growth.

Veblen and other precursors of evolutionary thinking in economics gave us the basic notion that an economy's institutions would allow it (if successful) to self-select in an ongoing way into the things it could do well, and hence to develop.[94] Behind this is the notion that no institutional arrangements resolve all problems for good. Ongoing adjustment of the rules governing investment, entrepreneurship and the regulation of labor markets are necessary as an economy undergoes structural change in the course of development (what are good institutional forms at one stage are no longer appropriate at others) and as external circumstances change.[95] Problem-solving coalitions and processes are necessary.

These three broad features and their associated economic behaviors characterize a wide variety of successful long-term economic development experiences. By contrast, cases of stagnation or long-term developmental regress manifest failure to achieve these features and to enjoy the microeconomic and aggregate effects described in Figure 3.

Figure 4 now shows how each of these types of incentive is shaped and given concrete institutional form by society-community interactions (horizontal), and in turn on their mutual interactions (vertical). The crux of our argument is shown in the fourth and fifth columns.

---

[92] Joel Mokyr, *The lever of riches: technological creativity and economic progress* (New York: Oxford University Press, 1990).

[93] Alesina and Rodrik, 'Distributive politics and economic growth' *op. cit.*; Persson and Tabellini, Political economics *op. cit.*

[94] Geoffrey Hodgson, *Reconstructing institutional economics: evolution, agency and structure in American institutionalism* (Book manuscript, University of Hertfordshire, 2002).

[95] Jennifer Bremer and John Kasarda, 'The origins of terror', *The Milken Institute Review* 4, 4 (2002) 34-48.

INCENTIVES NECESSARY TO LONG-TERM DEVELOPMENT	PRINCIPAL MICRO-ECONOMIC EFFECTS OF EACH INCENTIVE	OPERATIONAL INSTITUTIONS: BEHAVIOR, ROUTINES, REGULARITIES	ROLE OF COMMUNITARIAN "BONDING" IN BRINGING ABOUT EACH INCENTIVE	ROLE OF SOCIETAL "BRIDGING" IN BRINGING ABOUT EACH INCENTIVE
MICRO-ECONOMIC: confidence ↓	- Reduces transactions costs - Reduces moral hazards - Raises expectations and efforts ↓	- Encourages Schumpeterian entrepreneur - Improves coordination of firm-firm transactions - Raises investment levels ↓ →	- Reputation effects, shared conventions, identities (depends on process of group formation) - overcome certain information problems in low-cost way (but can encourage rent-seeking) →	- Overarching rules promote transparency and limit rent-seeking, help to complete markets ←
SOCIAL POLICY: Effective and acceptable distributional tradeoffs ↓↓	- Precedent encourages ongoing 'sacrifices' in face of shocks (Rodrik) - Overcomes disincentive to participate and make effort (Aghion) ↓↓	- Raises investments in skills - Raises work and entrepre-neurial participation rates - Improves willingness to pay taxes (investment) ↓↓ →	- Voice and loyalty - Being in the same boat enhances acceptability - Membership may involve real forms of intra-group redistribution →	- Counteracts corporatism and distributional hold-ups - Standards of fairness and efficiency constrain group demands - Inter-group mobility (exit), disciplines groups ←
PROBLEM-SOLVING: successful ongoing conflict resolution	- Participation of groups is enhanced - Minimize rent-seeking from corporatism	- Better adjustment of rules governing entrepreneurship and labor markets - Intelligent ideas more likely to receive support as public policy - Coalitions can form, avoiding chaotic instability →	- Secure groups encourage coalition formation: voice that gets heard (but risk of P-A problems) →	- Limits to group power encourage compromise - Exit options, defection, make other coalitions possible, hence dynamically limit P-A problems ←

Legend:
→↓ : cumulative and/or one-way causal effect
→← : two-way interactions and feedbacks

Figure 4 Society-Community interactions and incentives

Generalized confidence emerges when the pervasive information problems, attendant moral hazards, and market failures of all modern economies are attenuated, especially in their most creative and innovative activities and sectors. Communities are low-cost ways of resolving these problems, by creating trust, reputation effects and shared conventions. No fully "societal" system – whether markets or administered, centralized bureaucracies – has ever succeeded in doing everything that communities can do in this regard. But communities can be prejudicial to economic development if they lead to rent-seeking; hence, they must be in a delicate and dynamic relationship with the forces that promote transparency, entry and exit, and limit rent-seeking, helping to complete markets where communities might stifle them. Generalized confidence, in other words, requires both society and community.

The same is true of the achievement of effective and acceptable distributional tradeoffs. These can neither be administered by a societal overseer, nor will they come about from the spontaneous interaction of different communities with each other (and certainly will not come about from the spontaneous interaction of individual agents). Communities are based on loyalty, and they can give voice to agents whose claims would otherwise go unheard by markets.[96] Moreover, group membership has the virtue of diffusing a sense of "being in the same boat," and those who are in the boat can contribute to a mutual sense that fairness has been achieved (as well as injustice and anger). In the former case, the acceptability of any distributional tradeoff is enhanced. Finally, communities – even in the most modern of economies – often have concrete effects on distributional matters. Families in some economies carry out income redistribution and smoothing, mobilize savings at low interest rates, and share work. But society is necessary as well, if undesirable forms of cronyism or enduring hierarchy are to be avoided. Competition and political interaction between groups counteract corporatism and distributional hold-ups; generalized standards of efficiency and fairness can constrain certain group demands and privileges; and inter-group mobility (the possibility of exit) can have disciplining effects on what groups do to obtain their piece of the pie.

Ongoing conflict resolution is, in many ways, the overall dynamic outcome of these other features of development. Resolving such conflicts involves, at the very least, adjustment of rules governing the vital center of the development process: entrepreneurship, labor markets, and investment. Effective problem-solving and institutional adaptation come about when it is difficult for groups to practice excessive corporatism and rent-seeking and when problem-solving bridges are built between the relevant groups. On the one hand, the community-based social bonds referred to above provide groups a certain degree of security, allowing them to be "at

---

[96] In the formal sense, scale lowers transactions costs and raises the payoffs to addressing preferences shared on a large scale.

the table" so that their voices can be heard, whether formally or in a more diffused manner. Societal forces described create limits to group power, parameters for their actions, so that the position of groups is not so secure that other coalitions are impossible. Participation of many different groups prevents them from practicing negative forms of exit (resignation or winner-take-all) from the problem-solving process. This helps avoid the twin dangers of "bad" stability in the form of interest-based but non-developmentalist (rent-seeking) coalitions, on one hand, or extreme instability, on the other.[97] Hence, there is less danger that intelligent ideas will be blocked out, because the principal interest groups have less ability and incentive to bind themselves to rigid, exclusively self-serving positions. This makes institutional learning more probable,[98] and even may allow ongoing revision of the most basic institutional infrastructure, such as legal principles, the system of political power-sharing, and other factors that influence political opportunity structures and hence the possibility for competing ideas to be heard.[99]

What exactly is this relationship between bonding and bridging, however? Notice that in each area, the ideal-type outcomes described above are based on a sort of bargain, where a favorable balance of society and community allows the positive effects of each to emerge, while each also acts as a check and balance on the potentially negative effects of the other, taken alone. Thus, together society and community permit actors to reduce transactions costs, limit moral hazards, and reduce rent-seeking, while also reducing the exercise of absolute power by any group and hence promoting competition and innovation. All are critical to the definition of the expectations of agents and hence how they identify and project their interests into the collective sphere.[100] A favorable balance comes about when the right mix of forms of participation exists.

Thus, society and community shape each other, but paradoxically they do so because of their independence from one another; each consists of different kinds of social practices and interactions, constituted at different spatial-temporal scales. Hence, for the purposes of a theory of the institutional bases of economic development, Putnam's categories, rather than being added together into a single index of social capital, may be better maintained separate, as their effects are offsetting or corrective. This is also why the tendency for the social sciences to

---

[97] Alesina *et al.*, 'Political instability and economic growth' *op. cit.*

[98] Haggard, Pathways from the periphery *op. cit.*

[99] Aghion *et al.*, 'Endogenous political institutions' *op. cit.*; Evans, Embedded autonomy *op. cit.*

[100] Although the principal-agent problem and impossibility theorem show us that even within a group, such tensions can exist. However, there is a major difference in degree of tension and hence in the intensity of relationships within groups and between groups. If this were not the case, bridges between groups would be transformed into bonds within groups as different groups of principals merged and decided to have unified agents working for them.

become partisans of either society or community as the source of development is very likely wrong and why we argue here for a reformulation of the problem of the social foundations of the institutions that promote economic development.

This approach should help explain degrees of success in long-term economic development. Roughly speaking, we expect that bonding without bridging or bridging without bonding lead to the less desirable outcomes described in the NW and SE cases in Figure 5. Some kind of interaction between the two is most favorable to creating the incentives to long-term economic development.

SOCIETY	COMMUNITY	
	LOW	HIGH
HIGH	<ul><li>Insufficient public goods</li><li>Lower confidence, higher transactions costs</li><li>Long-term, unacceptable distributional tradeoffs</li><li>Costly conflict resolution, confrontational society</li></ul>	<ul><li>Facilitates confidence</li><li>Facilitates sustainable distributional trade offs</li><li>Facilitates conflict resolution</li><li>Strong society modernizes community</li><li>Strong community reduces costs associated with anonymity</li></ul>
LOW	<ul><li>Chaos</li><li>Law of the Jungle</li></ul>	<ul><li>Prevalence of "primitive" forms of community</li><li>Hierarchical relations between groups</li><li>Rent-seeking groups</li><li>Low-trust, lack of confidence</li><li>Unacceptable distributional effects due to rents and hierarchy</li><li>Permanent conflicts</li></ul>

Figure 5 The many possibilities[101]

5. Conclusion: Social forces, politics and economics

The notion that there are complex contexts for action such as those resulting from interaction of society and communities meets with significant resistance from most economic theory, which generally prefers to consider only societal forces – transparent and anonymous market-style relations between economic agents. These forces, by sustaining the whip of competition, effectively negate or render transitory

---

[101] I owe this figure to Andrés Rodríguez-Pose. See also Andrés Rodríguez-Pose, 'Instituciones y desarrollo económico', *Ciudad y Territorio: Estudios Territoriales* 31 (122) (1999) pp. 775-84.

and insignificant the possible roles for complex contexts. Even much contemporary institutional economics considers institutional forms to arise as a consequence of a set of market imperfections or information imperfections; thus, rational action generates institutional forms within the economy. As such its primary mission is not to analyze institutional contexts as *shapers of* the economy.[102] Comparative economics goes beyond this, in its "recognition that the pure competitive model is not a useful way to think about capitalist economies, and that political and economic institutions crucially shape performance"[103]. In contrast to institutional economics, which stresses the universal and common institutional foundations of modern economies, comparative economics emphasizes institutional diversity.[104] It shares with public choice theory an interest in political processes, but unlike the latter, admits that a wide variety of political and social factors will affect the choice of institutions and their efficiency. Comparative economics asks why certain institutional forms come about under different exogenous conditions, concluding that the latter set up particular bargaining or choice situations. Subsequent development can be seen as path dependent. Thus, for example, the existence of different communities (regional, ethnic, or feudal) affect the construction of institutional forms of property rights and the rule of law, which emerge because of the particular bargaining games between such groups. These institutions then have long-term effects on economic development because of the ways they affect individual incentives and collective problem-solving.

Nonetheless, comparative economics does not tell us clearly whether diversity merely reflects efficient solutions to different starting points, or whether there are many different equally efficient institutions for a given purpose. Moreover, comparative economics mostly focuses on "big" institutions, especially property rights and the rule of law. Most of its work is not on gradual improvements in institutions, small institutional practices, or institutions below the national level, the practical quotidian substance of democratic practice and its relationship to the development process. Thus, a double diversity is at work, not merely having to do with starting points, but also with different ways to resolve the collective action situations generated by starting points.

A number of these dilemmas of institutional analysis can be confronted by focusing on the interaction of society and community in defining the landscape of

---

[102] Edward L. Glaeser and Andre Shleifer, 'Legal origins' (Cambridge, MA: NBER Working Paper No. w8272, May 2001) *www.nber.org/papers/w8272*.

[103] Shleifer, 'The new comparative economics' *op. cit.*, p. 12.

[104] Institutionalist economics, in this sense, refers principally to transaction-cost economics, which are centrally interested in whether the conditions for Coasian bargains exist and if they do not, how to secure them, and when they do, what kinds of optimal institutional arrangements exist for a given problem.

incentives in the economy. A richer and more realistic palette of influences on action (notably those of community) can thus be taken into account than can be accommodated in most comparative economics, institutional economics, and public choice theory. This is because society and community interactions define the complex contexts alluded to above, with different starting points, but also with different possible efficient institutional forms for development. Society and community can interact in many efficient ways (not necessarily pareto efficient), such that the concrete institutional forms of confidence, distributional arrangements, and coalitional behavior which lead to development are many and sundry and they lead to complex evolutionary selection dynamics of economies into what they do best. But economies also fail: a workable balance between society and community – and thus the creation of solid incentives to development – is often not achieved, and this framework can be used to illuminate such failure.

Moreover, if the argument made in previous sections is correct, then there is no simple mapping of associational patterns or institutional forms onto success and failure, but rather the question of how institutions substantively resolve society-community relations. Along these lines, Rodrik and Engermann and Sokoloff show that there are many different ways to satisfy neoclassical development tenets;[105] good institutions deliver first-order development conditions effectively but not necessarily in identical ways. The task of our theory is thus not to search for consistent institutional forms – a putative isomorphism of institutions to development – but rather to find context-sensitive "razor's edge" interactions between bonding and bridging that achieve the substantive outcomes identified in economic theory and evidence.

The central proposition of this paper requires much more analytical precision and theoretical elaboration than we are able to give it here. While it is likely never to be as analytically parsimonious as certain other theories of the institutional foundations of development, it does respond to the need to reintroduce a realistic view of social forces into the theory of comparative economics, i.e. to relax the overly-restrictive assumptions which are commonly used in political economy and institutional economics to theorize economic development. It is nonetheless still relatively parsimonious because it locates sources of variety in the interaction of two basic forms of social organization, community and society.

Current debates over development theory and policy, however, show just how far away we are from any such sense of the problem. Market fundamentalists and institutionalists debate each other with little common language, with the former claiming the high ground of incentives but losing sight of how they are really

---

[105] Rodrik, 'Growth strategies' *op. cit.*; Stanley L. Engerman and Kenneth L. Sokoloff, 'Institutional and non-institutional explanations of economic differences' (Cambridge, MA: NBER Working Paper No. w9989, September 2003) *www.nber.org/papers/w9989*.

constructed, while the latter tend to emphasize control and authority over the development process and needlessly concede incentives and micro-efficiency to the context-less analyses of market fundamentalists.

The task proposed is complicated by the fact that the starting points for each society are different, and that the ending points, in terms of the precise articulations between society and community which are achievable and which correspond to the desires of each society, also show considerable variation. This in no way calls for complete relativism; it does help place the lessons from certain valuable parsimonious economic theories into a more grounded and realistic sociological framework.

BUZZ: FACE–TO–FACE CONTACT AND THE URBAN ECONOMY

Buzz: face-to-face contact and the urban economy[*]

MICHAEL STORPER and ANTHONY J. VENABLES

1. Face-to-face contact remains important

Face-to-face contact remains central to coordination of the economy, despite the remarkable reductions in transport costs and the astonishing rise in the complexity and variety of information – verbal, visual and symbolic – which can be communicated near instantly. Over the past quarter century, long-distance business travel has grown faster than output and trade.[1] There must be powerful reasons for economic agents to congregate and see each other, given the relatively high pecuniary and opportunity cost of business travel. Forces of urbanization and localization remain strong. For example, the geographical density of employment in many sectors in the US has actually increased in recent years.[2] It has also been estimated that, in the US, 380 localized clusters of firms employ 57% of the total workforce and generate 61% of the nation's output and fully 78% of its exports.[3] Other researchers, using more conservative measures, still find that 30% of the US workforce is accounted for by localized employment clusters.[4] Urbanization is continuing apace in developing countries, and many cities in high-income countries are experiencing a resurgence.[5]

Three main forces are thought to lie behind the persistence of urbanization and localization: backward and forward linkages of firms, including access to markets; the clustering of workers; and localized interactions which promote technological

---

[*] Earlier versions of this paper were presented at the International Seminar on Economy and Space, Faculty of Economics, Federal University of Minas Gerais (FACE/UFMG), Centre for Regional Development and Planning (CEDEPLAR), Ouro Preto, Minas Gerais, Brazil, December 6-7, 2001; as keynote address to the Third International Congress on the Dynamics of Proximity, Paris, December 2001; to the Center for Globalization and Policy Studies, UCLA, March 2002; and to the DRUID Summer Conference, June 2003. This paper will also be published in the *Journal of Economic Geography*.

[1] Peter Hall, *Cities in civilization* (London: Weidenfeld & Nicolson, 1998).

[2] Sukkoo Kim, 'The reconstruction of the American urban landscape in the twentieth century' (Cambridge, MA: NBER Working Paper No. w8857, March 2002) *www.nber.org/papers/w8857*.

[3] Stuart A. Rosenfeld, 'United States: business clusters', in OECD, *Networks of enterprises and local development* (Paris: Organisation for Economic Cooperation and Development, Territorial Development Service, 1996) pp. 179-202.

[4] Michael E. Porter, 'Clusters of innovation: regional foundations of competitiveness' (Washington, DC: US Council on Competitiveness, 2001).

[5] Allen J. Scott (ed.) *Global city regions: theory and policy* (Oxford: Oxford University Press, 2001).

innovation. We argue in this paper that analysis of these mechanisms is likely to be incomplete unless grounded in the most fundamental aspect of proximity: face-to-face contact (F2F).

To begin with, there is widespread agreement that localized backward and forward linkages, while important in specific cases, can account for only a small part of contemporary urbanization.[6] More importantly, when such linkages are strongly localized, it is rarely because of high physical transport costs, and frequently because the information associated with the physical transaction is costly or difficult to transmit at great distance. Deal-making, evaluation and relationship adjustment are heavily dependent on face-to-face contact.

The clustering of workers is considered to be a strong contributor to localization and urbanization, largely because of the increasing demand for specialized skills and more flexible, higher turnover labor markets. Taken together, they place a premium on clustering because employers thereby gain access to a large pool of specialized labor and can avoid hoarding during downturns. Workers gain access to a greater number of potential employers, allowing them to minimize periods of unemployment and make more rapid progression up a career ladder, with greater lifetime learning and wage growth.[7] Underpinning these dynamics, however, are detailed processes of signaling and screening which occur largely through face-to-face contact, as well as network structures that are constructed through such contact.[8]

The third group of explanations concern technological innovation. There is fragmentary but fairly convincing evidence that cities are centers of innovation in the production of ideas and knowledge and in their commercialization.[9] The notion frequently adduced to explain these facts is that spatial proximity must somehow improve flows of information upon which innovators depend, creating technological "spillovers". However, the mechanisms underlying these spillovers remain unclear. One avenue of inquiry has to do with the circulation of knowledgeable workers between firms, enhancing the ability of these firms to recombine knowledge, imitate best practices, and otherwise improve their products. For example, in Glaeser's

---

[6] Ian R. Gordon and Philip McCann, 'Industrial clusters: complexes, agglomeration, and/or social networks?', *Urban Studies* 37 (2000) pp. 513-32.

[7] Julio J. Rotemberg and Garth Saloner, 'Competition and human capital accumulation: a theory of inter-regional specialisation and trade', *Regional Science and Urban Economics* 30 (2000) pp. 373-404; H. Jayet, 'Chômer plus souvent en région urbaine, plus longtemps en région rurale', *Economie et Statistique* 153 (1983) pp. 47-57.

[8] Mark Granovetter, *Getting a job: a study in contacts and careers* (Chicago: University of Chicago Press, 1986).

[9] Maryann P. Feldman and David B. Audretsch, 'Innovation in cities: science-based diversity, specialization, and localized competition', *European Economic Review* 43 (1999) pp. 409-29; Adam B. Jaffe, Manuel Trajtenberg and Rebecca Henderson, 'Geographic localization of knowledge spillovers as evidenced by patent citations', *Quarterly Journal of Economics* 63 (1993) pp. 577-98.

model of learning,[10] people can absorb knowledge from contact with more skilled individuals in their own industry, and the number of probable contacts an individual makes is an increasing function of city size. Large cities therefore facilitate learning, and are particularly attractive for highly-talented young people who have large potential returns from learning. The hypothesis is therefore, that knowledge "rubs off" on people in places such as Silicon Valley or the City of London. But if this is the case, it is through F2F that rubbing off occurs, and we require a theory of the motivations people have for engaging in F2F.

Jacobs advanced the idea that cities enjoy an advantage because of their economic and social diversity.[11] This diversity, because it is highly packed into limited space, facilitates haphazard, serendipitous contact among people. Florida,[12] drawing on the classical notions of Simmel and Tönnies,[13] argues that the diversity found in cosmopolitan cities facilitates "creativity" because of the openness of their networks, the liberating force of anonymity and hence resistance to hide-bound tradition. But in none of these formulations can be found a direct explanation of the F2F interaction by which cosmopolitanism and diversity have their positive effects. Nor do these approaches consider the disadvantages of anonymity and large numbers, in the form of the costs to coordination they may generate, or the way in which the economy overcomes these difficulties.[14]

In another vein, Alfred Marshall, one of the main inspirations for contemporary students of the "industrial district," also suggested the importance of direct and unplanned contact between economic agents.[15] Marshall centers on belonging to a specialised producer community which diffuses the "secrets" of industry, not the kind of cosmopolitan and haphazard city life described by Jacobs. Numerous attempts have been made to transform his notion into a theory of the milieux underlying contemporary industrial districts. All beg the question: if agents belong to a mileu, what do their interactions consist of and what are the incentives for undertaking such interactions?

---

[10] Edward L. Glaeser, 'Learning in cities', *Journal of Urban Economics* 46 (1999) pp. 254-77.

[11] Jane Jacobs, *The economy of cities* (New York: Random House, 1969).

[12] Richard Florida, *The rise of the creative class* (New York: Basic Books, 2002).

[13] Georg Simmel, *The sociology of Georg Simmel* (Glencoe, IL: The Free Press, 1950).

[14] Although the classical arguments in sociology were concerned precisely with the negative effects of the modern urban social order in the form of their notion of anomie. While sociology does have a notion of the compensating forms of "social integration" that might aid modern anonymous actors to become part of a society, it does not ask how actors might "coordinate" in the face of anonymity and large numbers.

[15] Alfred Marshall, *Principles of economics* (London: Macmillan, 8th ed. 1919); Giacomo Becattini, *Il distretto industriale: un nuovo modo di interpretare il cambiamento economico* (Turin: Rosenberg & Sellier, 2000).

In sum, the various theories of agglomeration and the persistence of cities refer to transactional structures and circumstances that necessitate close contact between persons, and to the various outcomes of proximity between agents – more effective input-output linkages, more effective labor market matching, technological spillovers. However, they do not explain precisely what individuals do in this form of encounter, nor why they do it. These encounters are, of course, face-to-face contacts between economic agents. F2F is thus a missing aspect of mechanisms that are considered to generate agglomeration.

This paper contributes to the understanding of F2F contact. First, we show that F2F has unique behavioral and communicational properties which give it specific advantages as a technology of communication, coordination, and motivation (§2). We develop two game-theoretic models which illustrate why agents engage in F2F contact and contribute some building blocks of a micro-economic theory of F2F (§3). We then place these ideas in the wider context of the role of F2F, amongst other mechanisms, in coordinating activity in different areas of the economy (§4). Finally, we offer concluding remarks on the future importance of F2F.

2. The specific properties of face-to-face contact

In order to consider the possible role of F2F in the economy, its properties as a type of behavior and interaction need to be identified. Table 1 lists four major properties of F2F contact: it is an efficient communication technology; it allows actors to align commitments and thereby reduces incentive problems; it allows screening of agents; and it motivates effort.

FUNCTION	ADVANTAGE OF F2F	CONTEXT
Communication technology	High frequency Rapid feedback Visual and body language cues	Non-codifiable information R&D Teaching
Trust and incentives in relationships	Detection of lying Co-presence a commitment of time	Meetings
Screening and socializing	Loss of anonymity Judging and being judged Acquisition of shared values	Professional groups Being 'in the loop'
Rush and motivation	Performance as display	Presentations

Table 1 Face-to-face contact

2.1 F2F contact as a communication technology

The first row of Table 1 refers to the advantages of F2F as a *communication technology*, particularly when much of the information to be transmitted cannot be codified.

Codifiable information has a stable meaning which is associated in a determinate way with the symbol system in which it is expressed, whether it be linguistic, mathematical, or visual. Such information is cheap to transfer because its underlying symbol systems can be widely disseminated through information infrastructure, sharply reducing the marginal cost of individual messages. Acquiring the symbol system may be expensive or slow (language, mathematical skills, etc.), as may be building the transmission system, but using it to communicate information is cheap. Thus, the transmission of codifiable information has strong network externalities, since once the infrastructure is acquired a new user can plug in and access the whole network.

By contrast, uncodifiable information is only loosely related to the symbol system in which it is expressed. This includes much linguistic, words-based expression (the famous distinction between "speech" and "language"), particularly what might be called "complex discourse".[16] For example, one can master the grammar and the syntax of a language without understanding its metaphors. This is also true for some mathematically expressed information, and much visual information. If the information is not codifiable, merely acquiring the symbol system or having the physical infrastructure is not enough for the successful transmission of a message. Transmission of uncodifable information may have very limited network externalities, since the successful transmission of the message depends on infrastructure that is largely committed to one specific sender-receiver pair. Bateson refers to the "analog" quality of tacit knowledge:[17] communication between individuals which requires a kind of parallel processing of the complexities of an issue, as different dimensions of a problem are perceived and understood only in relation to one another.

F2F encounters provide an efficient technology of transaction under these circumstances, by permitting a depth and speed of feedback that is impossible in other forms of communication. As organizational theorists Nitin Nohria and Robert Eccles point out:

> ...relative to electronically-mediated exchange, the structure of face-to-face interaction offers an unusual capacity for interruption, repair, feedback, and learning. In contrast to interactions that are largely sequential, face-to-face interaction makes it possible for two people to be

---

[16] John R. Searle, *Speech acts: an essay in the philosophy of language* (New York: Cambridge University Press, 1969).

[17] Gregory Bateson, *Steps to an ecology of mind* (London: Paladin Press, 1973).

sending and delivering messages simultaneously. The cycle of interruption, feedback and repair possible in face-to-face interaction is so quick that it is virtually instantaneous.[18]

This echoes the findings of sociologist Goffman that "a speaker can see how others are responding to her message even before it is done and alter it midstream to elicit a different response."[19]

But it is not just the uncodifiability of much information that makes F2F a superior technology. Communication in an F2F context occurs on many levels at the same time – verbal, physical, contextual, intentional, and non-intentional. Such multidimensional communication is held by many to be essential to the transmission of complex, tacit knowledge. For example, social psychologists argue that creativity results from several different ways of processing information at one time, including not only the standard deductive way but analogical, metaphorical, and parallel methods as well.[20] These different means of communication are mutually enriching, and lead to connections being made that cannot be had through strictly linear perception and reasoning. An extension of this is that the full benefits of diversity and serendipity are only realized through these multiple levels of communication. Linguists such as Searle and Austin develop another aspect of communicational analysis, arguing that "language is behavior" and F2F dialogue is a complex socially-creative activity.[21] In a similar vein, sociologists such as Goffman and Garfinkel show that the interaction which comes from co-presence can be likened to being on stage, playing a role, where the visual and corporeal cues are at least as important to knowing what is being "said" as are the words themselves.[22]

2.2 Trust and incentives in relationships[23]

The second row of Table 1 refers to the notion that co-presence may reduce incentive and coordination problems that arise in economic relationships. With tacit knowledge there is always residual uncertainty and hence the need to minimize the

---

[18] Nitin Nohria and Robert G. Eccles, *Networks and organizations: structure, form and action* (Boston: Harvard Business School Press, 1992) p. 292.

[19] Erving Goffman, *Interaction ritual: essays on face-to-face behavior* (New York: Pantheon Books, 1982).

[20] Bateson, Steps to an ecology of mind *op. cit.*; Mihaly Csikszentmihalyi, *Creativity: flow and the psychology of discovery and invention* (New York: Harper Collins, 1996).

[21] Searle, Speech acts *op. cit.*; John L. Austin, *How to do things with words* (Oxford: Clarendon Press, 1962).

[22] Erving Goffman, *The presentation of self in everyday life* (New York: Doubleday, 1959); Harold Garfinkel, *Studies in ethnomethodology* (Oxford: Blackwell, 1987).

[23] This section draws from Edward E. Leamer and Michael Storper, 'The economic geography of the Internet Age', *Journal of International Business Studies* 32 (2001) pp. 641-65, and NBER Working Paper No. W8450 (Cambridge, MA, August 2001) *www.nber.org/papers/w8450*.

incentives for one agent to free ride or manipulate the other. These moral hazards exist when the inherent degree of reliability of a message is low. They can sometimes be reduced through improvements in the transparency or clarity of the information itself or in how well it can be verified. But in other cases they require shaping a relationship between the interested parties. Being close enough literally to touch each other allows visual "contact" and "emotional closeness," the basis for building human relationships.

For example, the contemporary knowledge-based economy involves many projects in which individuals come together to acquire and exchange information. Typically the later stages of such a project – writing the report, executing the transaction, or constructing the investment – involve codifiable information. It is the earlier stages where information is more fluid. Is the project a good idea? Should one approach be followed or another? Answering these questions requires that partners in the project undertake research and share their results. Often neither the inputs nor the outputs of this research are observable. Thus, a partner can conscientiously research the project or simply free-ride, hoping that other members of the team will do the work.

F2F can play important roles in mitigating these incentive and free-rider problems. One reason for this is simply that it is easier to observe and intepret a partner's behavior in an F2F situation. Any message may be understood but not believed. There are strong questions of intentionality at work in communication. Knowing the intentions of another actor enables us to decode the practical consequences of what they are expressing to us.[24] Speech and action are tightly interrelated, but speech does not automatically reveal to us what another person intends to do .[25] Humans are very effective at sensing non-verbal messages from one another, particularly about emotions, cooperation, and trustworthiness. Putnam notes that "it seems that the ability to spot non-verbal signs of mendacity offered a significant survival advantage during the course of human evolution."[26] Psychologist Albert Mehrabian notes that "our facial and vocal expressions, postures, movements and gestures," are crucial; when our words "contradict the messages contained within them, others mistrust what we say – they rely almost completely on what we do."[27]

A second reason is that F2F may promote the development of trust. Trust depends on reputation effects or on multi-layered relations between the parties to a

---

[24] Edmund Husserl, *The idea of phenomenology* (The Hague: Nijhoff, 1968).

[25] Searle, Speech acts *op. cit.*

[26] Robert D. Putnam, *Bowling alone: the collapse and revival of American community* (New York: Simon and Schuster, 2000) p. 175.

[27] Albert Mehrabian, *Silent messages: implicit communications of emotions and attitudes* (Belmont, CA: Wadsworth, 1981) p. iii.

transaction that can create low-cost enforcement opportunities.[28] Trust also comes from the fact that partners expend time, money and effort in building a relationship. The time and money costs of co-presence (schmoozing) can be substantial, far outweighing the cost of the message. These costs are sunk, so indicate a willingness to embark on a repeated relationship; absent a second date, the value of the first date disappears. However, to create a relationship bond, the costs must be substantial and transparent. E-mail, paradoxically, can be so efficient that it destroys the value of the message. The e-mail medium greatly reduces the cost of sending a message, somewhat reduces the cost of receiving the message, and it makes the costs mostly nontransparent. The low costs and the nontransparency greatly limit the value of the relationship bond. A return receipt only means that the recipient has opened the message, but the sender cannot be sure that enough attention has been devoted to it to absorb the content. In this sense, for complex context-dependent information, the medium *is* the message. And the most powerful such medium for verifying the intentions of another is direct F2F contact.

2.3 Screening and socialization

Even if we admit, on the basis of the above argument, that F2F is an efficient technology of transacting, it is nonetheless very costly, not least because it is time consuming. We do not have the luxury of F2F encounters with the entire world, so need to screen out the people with whom we want to interact. How do we identify such people? One way is formal screening procedures – examination and certification. Another is the development of informal networks, in which members of the network develop and share a pool of knowledge about members' competence.

Social and professional networks of this type often – although not always – require F2F contact. One reason is that they are necessarily based on individuals losing their anonymity; a member of the group is continually judging other members of the group, being judged, and sharing judgements with members of the group. In some internationalised professions – such as academia – this does not always require co-location, although is certainly reinforced by F2F in the conference circuit. In other activities these information networks can only be maintained within a restricted geographical area. In such fields as fashion, public relations, and many of the arts (including cinema, television, and radio) there are international networks "at the top," but in the middle of these professions networks are highly localised, change rapidly, and information used by members to stay in the loop is highly context-dependent. In

---

[28] Diego Gambetta (ed.) *Trust: making and breaking cooperative relations* (Oxford: Blackwell, 1988); Edward H. Lorenz, 'Trust, community, and cooperation: toward a theory of industrial districts', in Michael Storper and Allen J. Scott (eds.) *Pathways to industrialization and regional development* (London: Routledge, 1992) pp. 195-204.

parts of the financial services and high technology industries, local networks intersect with long-distance contact systems. In almost anything relating to business-government relations, networks have a strongly national and regional cast.

The screening of network members and potential partners is complex because much of what is most valuable about partners is their tacit knowledge. Much of such knowledge can only be successfully communicated as metaphor,[29] whose meanings are highly culture and context-dependent.[30] Polanyi argued that tacit and metaphorical knowledge is deeply embedded in specific contexts.[31] Thus, potential partners need to 'know' each other, or have a broad common background, acquired through socialization. Sociological theory refers to socialization as the production of the individual as a social being who develops specific capacities to signal to others that she belongs to a certain world, and hence elicits from others the recognition of belonging.[32] Individuals learn to share the "codes" which show that they have certain criteria of judgement, which in turn signal to others that they belong to the same social world.[33] This gives them the means to become members of structured milieux, to get "in the loop." Socialization is inevitably achieved in large measure through face-to-face contact, from family, schooling, and the social environment in one's community and workplaces.

Notice, then, that F2F performs its screening role at two timescales in the economic process: in the long-run, by socializing people; in the short–run, by permitting potential collaborators to evaluate others' performance in professional groups and networks.

2.4 "Rush" and the motivation that comes from F2F contact

The final row of Table 1 shows another dimension of the incentive effects of F2F contact, which goes beyond verbal or visual communication. F2F communication does not derive its richness and power merely from allowing us to see each other's faces and to detect the intended and unintended messages that can be sent by such

---

[29] Robert Nisbet, *Social change and history: aspects of the Western theory of development* (Oxford: Oxford University Press, 1969).

[30] George Lakoff and Mark Johnson, *Metaphors we live by* (Chicago: University of Chicago Press, 1980).

[31] Michael Polanyi, *The tacit dimension* (London: Routledge, 1966) p. 4.

[32] The concept of socialization belongs upstream of economists' notions of human capital, screening and selection, because it is concerned with generation of initial capacities for action and discrimination, not merely their rational deployment. See George A. Akerlof and Rachel E. Kranton, 'Economics and identity', *Quarterly Journal of Economics* 115 (2000) pp. 715-53, for models of the economics of group identity.

[33] James S. Coleman, *Foundations of social theory* (Cambridge, MA: Harvard/ Belknap, 1990).

visual contact. As noted, according to Goffman,[34] F2F communication is a *performance*, a means to information production and not merely to more efficient exchange. In this performance, speech, intentions, role-playing and a specific context all come together to raise the quantity and quality of information which can be transmitted. Moreover, performance raises effort by stimulating imitation and competition. Psychologists have shown that the search for pleasure is a powerful motivating force in behavior, and certain kinds of pleasure are linked to pride of status and position: we imitate others, try to do better than them and derive pleasure from succeeding at so doing. When we make an effort, and are on the route to success, there is a bio-physical "rush" that pushes us forward. However, all pleasure quickly recedes as it blends into the preceding "normal" state, and it is only by once again changing this state that pleasure is found again. The search for such pride of status and position is thus a strong motivation which must be continuously renewed.[35] F2F contact provides the strongest, most embodied signals of such desire and can generate the rush that pushes us to make greater and better efforts. It is thus no surprise that even with the sophisticated computer monitoring that can be carried out on employee performance today, very few workplaces – which are essentially centers of F2F contact – have disappeared. It is not just that it is easier to monitor employees when they are present, it is also that such presence is motivating, because it contributes to desire, imitation, and competition, and the fear of shame from failure.[36]

3. Why people engage in F2F: two models

With these basic properties of F2F contact in mind, we now propose two analytical models of how F2F improves the coordination of economic agents. In the first, F2F overcomes incentive problems in the formation of working partnerships; in the second, it allows actors to evaluate others' qualities and leads to the formation of "in groups" that support more efficient partnering and increased motivation. These models begin the task of developing a micro-economic theory of F2F. They both yield the result that productivity is raised by F2F contact.

---

[34] Goffman, The presentation of self in everyday life *op. cit.*

[35] Tibor Scitovsky, *The joyless economy: an inquiry into human satisfaction and consumer dissatisfaction* (New York: Oxford University Press, 1976).

[36] Ibid.; Daniel Kahneman, Ed Diener and Norbert Schwarz (eds.) *Well-being: the foundations of hedonic psychology* (New York: Russell Sage Foundation, 1999).

3.1 Incentives in joint projects

Game theoretic analysis provides a way of drawing out some of the incentive issues that arise when information is fluid and actions are not observable. To illustrate, suppose that two people are considering undertaking a joint project, but they are uncertain about its ultimate value or quality. All they know, initially, is that the project is either good, yielding final payoff A, or bad, yielding zero; they both attach the same prior probability, ϱ, to the project being good. The game has two stages. The first involves acquisition of information about the quality of the project, and the second involves information sharing, deciding whether or not to undertake the project, and project implementation. What are the incentives to acquire information or to free-ride, and how might they be improved by F2F contact?

At the first stage the two individuals undertake research independently and obtain a signal of whether the project is good or bad. The signal obtained by player i may be favorable, g_i, or unfavorable, b_i. However, the signals are not accurate – a good project can send out a signal that it is bad, and vice versa. By expending effort, e_i, each player ($i = 1, 2$) can improve the quality of the signal received (details are given in Appendix 1).

At the second stage of the game players truthfully reveal their signals to each other.[37] Using standard Bayesian techniques they use their combined information to compute the probability that the project is good; this probability is higher the more good signals have been received and the more effort has been expended, improving the quality of the signals. They then decide whether or not to proceed. Proceeding costs C and yields payoff A if the project turns out to be good, and zero otherwise; we assume $A\varrho = C$, so (prior to research) the project yields zero expected surplus.

The incentives faced by individuals and the equilibrium outcomes are illustrated in Figure 1. The axes are the effort levels of the two players, and the lines OA and OB divide the space up into three regions. Between OA and OB effort levels are such that players will, at the second stage, choose to go ahead with the project only if they have both received good signals, $\{g_1, g_2\}$. However, below OB player 1 is putting in so little effort relative to player 2 (and hence 1's signal is so unreliable) that they proceed if 2 has a good signal and 1 a bad one $\{g_2, b_1\}$. Similarly, above OA they proceed with signals $\{g_1, b_2\}$. The curves labeled EU$_1$ are expected utility indifference curves for player 1, increasing to the right, and kinked where they cross lines OA and OB. The best response function for player 1 to each effort level e_2 is given by the bold solid lines, $e_1 = R_1(e_2)$. We see that if e_2 is very low, then player 1 will ignore 2's signal and put in a constant amount of effort (in the region to the left of OA).

---

[37] At this stage of the game there is no incentive for players to not reveal their true signal or the effort expended in obtaining the signal. A richer model might link the share of the project's surplus to effort, in which case there are incentives to misrepresent.

53

Conversely, if e_2 is high enough, player 1 will free-ride, putting in zero effort (in the region below OB). At intermediate levels of e_2 player 1 puts in a positive level of effort, decreasing in e_2. Just as the solid bold lines are the best responses of player 1 to 2's effort levels, so the dashed bold lines (their reflection around the 45° line) give the best responses of player 2 to 1's effort levels.

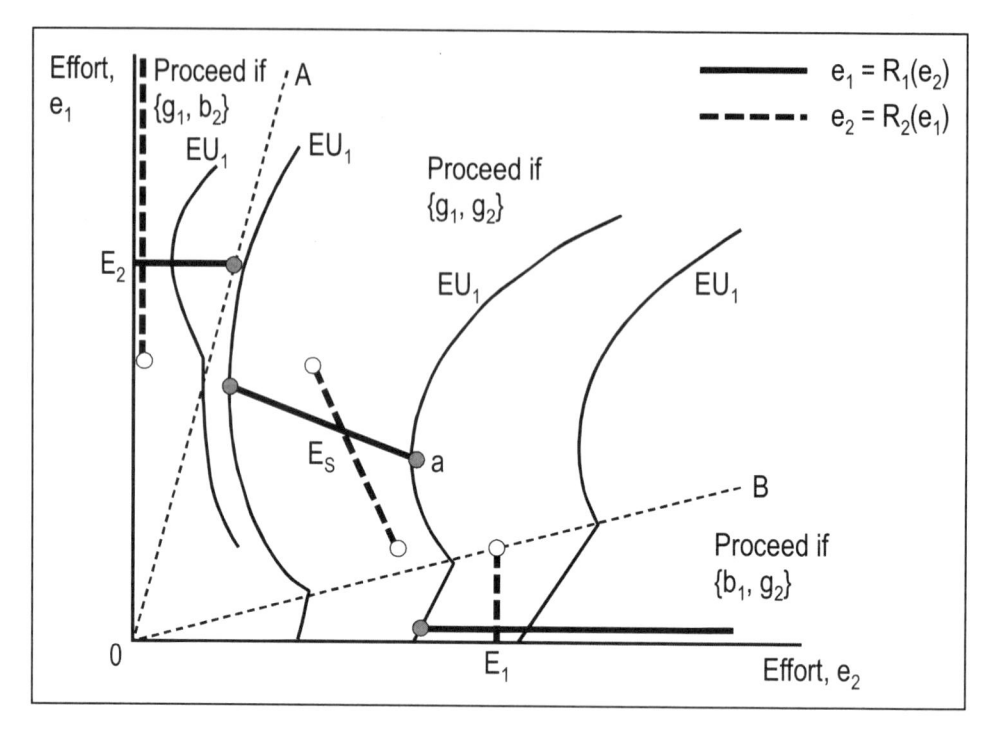

Figure 1 Equilibria in a game of information acquisition and sharing

As illustrated in Figure 1, this game has three Nash equilibria, labeled E_S, E_1 and E_2, occurring where the best response functions of the two players intersect. E_S is symmetric, and involves both players putting in equal amounts of effort. E_1 and E_2 are equilibria where player 1 (respectively 2) exerts no effort; but given this, it is privately optimal for the other player to put in effort to the level illustrated. This free-riding means that little information is gathered, and at these equilibria more projects are undertaken than at E_S, the proportion of failing projects is larger, and aggregate returns lower.[38]

---

[38] The game has a similar structure to 'chicken' in which two Californian kids drive towards each other. The last to swerve is the winner.

The multiplicity of equilibria reflects the incentives for individuals to free-ride in projects of this type. What can F2F do to select the symmetric equilibrium, where free-riding is reduced? F2F contact – a meeting between the players – can play two distinct roles. First, an F2F meeting prior to the start of the game may allow players to coordinate on this equilibrium. It is quite difficult to go into a meeting maintaining a commitment to put in no effort. This is partly because of the inherent simultaneity of the meeting: the two players are placed in a situation where neither has a mechanism to commit to making no effort. And it is partly because of the psychological effects of F2F contact; participants want to be highly esteemed by others and this is likely to be fostered by cooperation rather than conflict. With F2F it is thus difficult for one player to maintain the position that he will put in no effort and free ride on the other.

A second role that an F2F meeting can play derives from the fact that meetings are a relatively costly form of information exchange. Suppose that players can only exchange their information in a meeting. Attending the meeting has a real cost and, crucially, each player makes the decision of whether or not to attend on the basis of her *own* information: it is in the meeting that information is shared and the decision on whether or not to go ahead with the project is taken. How does this change the situation, as compared to costless information sharing? If the meeting cost is high enough then players who have done no research (as well as those who have received an unfavorable signal) will not find it worthwhile to attend the meeting. As a consequence, doing nothing is no longer privately profitable; each player has to pay a cost (that of attending the meeting) before obtaining the partner's information, and the cost is not worth paying given the original information.

In terms of Figure 1, there is a change in the shape of each player's indifference curves. Critically, below OB it is no longer worthwhile for player 1 to turn up to the meeting if his signal is bad. In this event there is no prospect of sharing surplus from the project, reducing EU_1 in the region below OB, compared to above. This change in the shape of the EU_1 indifference curves means that the best response function $R(e_2)$ is extended to the right from point *a*. Extending it sufficiently far, point E_1 (and similarly E_2) cease to be equilibria. The best response functions now have a single intersection at E_S where both players have positive effort levels. The meeting therefore reduces the set of equilibria to the unique one at which both players make an effort.

This analysis, while highly stylized, formalizes two different possible roles that F2F meetings may have. One is as a form of preplay communication to coordinate on one of the possible equilibria. The other is as a way of increasing the cost of free-riding; a player who makes no effort will not find it worthwhile to attend the meeting, and so cannot make a positive return from the project.[39]

3.2 The formation of in-groups: getting into the loop

We argued in section 2.3 that prior screening or socialization of potential partners is important. In many contexts this can be provided by formal certification and institutionalised screening mechanism, such as professional examinations. However, in other contexts – particularly in creative activities where ability is hard to formally assess and where performance criteria cannot be codified and institutionalised – such formal techniques may not be very useful. Instead informal networks – being 'in the loop' or in the 'in-group' – may take their place as screening mechanisms.

What is the informational basis of such a group? Where ex ante screening and certification of individuals' ability or effort is not possible there has to be open, although not necessarily costless, membership to all. However, once in, members cease to be anonymous, knowing who is in the group, observing the performance of members, and in turn being observed by other members. This information is used to maintain the quality of the group. At its simplest, a record of failure is used as the basis for expulsion from the group. Group members are therefore continually judging and being judged, and know exactly who is 'in' and who is 'out'.

If an in-group of this type forms it will have a number of characteristics. First, it will contain a higher than average proportion of able people; high ability people have a higher probability of undertaking successful projects, so are more likely to survive as members of the group. Second, members of the group will (conditional on their ability) have higher earnings than outsiders, because they are matching with (on average) higher quality people. Third, members of the group will work harder than outsiders; the earnings differential creates an incentive to stay in the group, and the probability of staying in is increased by hard work. Finally, although initial access to the group is open to all, there may be an entry cost, perhaps in the form of time and effort to become known as deserving to belong to the group. Even if this is the same for people of all abilities it will have a greater deterrent effect for the less able because their income gain from being in the group is less. This is a further self-selection mechanism that reinforces the ability composition of the in-group relative to outsiders.[40]

---

[39] Notice that this meeting is about information sharing, not about collective decision taking. In the latter context Osborne *et al.* argue that meeting costs can reduce the quality of decision taking by reducing attendance; Martin J. Osborne, Jeffrey S. Rosenthal and Matthew A. Turner, 'Meetings with costly participation', *American Economic Review* 90 (2000) pp. 927-43.

[40] The model lies, in broad terms, in the class of models of neighborhood formation – interactions occur between individuals in endogenously formed groups. Such models are surveyed by Steven

To model this, suppose that there is a population of size one, with exogenous death and birth rate of δ per period. The population contains two types of individual, high ability and low ability, subscripted by H and L, and the proportion of high ability in the population is $\bar{\mu}$. The size of the in-group is endogenously determined and denoted φ. The proportion of this group that is of high ability (also endogenous) is denoted μ^I, while the proportion of outsiders that are high ability is μ^O, so $\bar{\mu} = \mu^I \phi + \mu^O (1-\phi)$ where we use superscripts I and O to denote variables for insiders and outsiders respectively.

In each time period all individuals match into pairs to undertake a project. Matching takes place *within* each group, but is otherwise random. The success or failure of a project depends on the ability of the two partners and the effort they put in, so the probabilities of success for projects with two high ability partners, a high ability partner and a low ability partner, or two low ability partners takes the following forms, for $i = O, I$:

$$\pi^i_{HH} = \rho_{HH} + f(e^i_H) + f(e^i_H),$$
$$\pi^i_{HL} = \rho_{HL} + f(e^i_H) + f(e^i_L), \qquad (1)$$
$$\pi^i_{LL} = \rho_{LL} + f(e^i_L) + f(e^i_L)$$

These probabilities depend on an exogenous component, $\rho_{HH} > \rho_{HL} > \rho_{LL}$, and on the effort of the individuals. We shall assume $\rho_{HH} - \rho_{HL} = \rho_{HL} - \rho_{LL}$, so that pairing with a high ability individual is as valuable for a low ability individual as it is for someone of high ability.[41] An individual's effort is denoted e^I_H for a high ability person inside the group, etc., and affects probability through an increasing concave function, $f(\ )$. Thus, a project is more likely to be successful if undertaken by high ability and harder working individuals.

If a project undertaken by members of the in-group fails, then both the participants in the project are ejected from the group with probability γ.[42] Since the probability of failing depends on one's partner, and partners are selected randomly from members of the group, the ejection probabilities for high and low ability people, η_H and η_L are given by,

$$\eta_H = \gamma \left[(1-\pi^i_{HH}) \mu^I + (1-\pi^i_{HL})(1-\mu^I) \right]$$

N. Durlauf, 'Neighborhood effects', forthcoming in J.V. Henderson and J.-F. Thisse (eds.) *Handbook of regional and urban economics* (Amsterdam: North-Holland, 2003). The spatial aspect of the present model derives from knowledge flows within a spatially concentrated group, the membership of which is determined primarily by ejection due to failing projects.

[41] A good match has the same effect on probability for high and low ability people. Adding super-modularity would reinforce results that follow, while sufficient sub-modularity could reverse them.

[42] This ejection probability is exogenous. In a more complex model it might depend on the full history of success and failure, rather than just success on the previous project.

$$\eta_L = \gamma\left[(1-\pi^i_{HL})\mu^I + (1-\pi^i_{LL})(1-\mu^I)\right] \tag{2}$$

Thus, the probability of an individual in the group matching with a high ability person is μ^I; a partnership with two high ability individuals fails with probability $(1-\pi^i_{HH})$ and a partnership with one high and one low ability individual fails with probability $(1-\pi^i_{HL})$, etc.

The size and skill composition of the in-group can now be determined. The number of able people in the in-group, $\phi\mu^I$, evolves according to differential equation

$$d(\phi\mu^I)/dt = \delta\bar{\mu}\lambda_H - (\eta_H + \delta)\phi\mu^I \tag{3}$$

The first term is the flow of able people going into the group. This consists of births, δ, proportion $\bar{\mu}$ of whom are able, and proportion λ_H of whom choose to enter the group (this proportion may be unity, and is discussed below). The second term is the number of high ability people who are ejected plus the number who die. Similarly, for low ability people,

$$d(\phi(1-\mu^I))/dt = \delta(1-\bar{\mu})\lambda_L - (\eta_L + \delta)\phi(1-\mu^I) \tag{4}$$

In steady state these expressions are zero, giving the numbers of high ability and low people in the in-group, $\phi\mu^I$ and $\phi(1 - \mu^I)$, as:

$$\phi\mu^I = \frac{\delta\bar{\mu}\lambda_H}{\eta_H + \delta}, \qquad \phi(1-\mu^I) = \frac{\delta(1-\bar{\mu})\lambda_L}{\eta_L + \delta} \tag{5}$$

Equations (1) - (5) give the base case model. If we suppose that all individuals have the same effort levels ($e^I_H = e^I_L = e^O_H = e^O_L$) and all members of the population start off in the group, $\lambda_H = \lambda_L = 1$, then it is easy to show that the in-group is of higher average ability than outsiders, $\mu^I > \mu^O$, simply because high ability people are less likely to be involved in failing projects and face ejection. The benefits from being in the group can be evaluated once we specify returns to project success or failure. Suppose then, that a successful project yields payoff 2α, an unsuccessful one yields 2β, and the payoff is split equally between the two partners. The expected payoffs to a high and low ability individual inside or outside ($i = I, O$) are given by,

$$u^i_H = \alpha\left[\pi^i_{HH}\mu^i + \pi^i_{HL}(1-\mu^i)\right] + \beta\left[(1-\pi^i_{HH})\mu^i + (1-\pi^i_{HL})(1-\mu^i)\right] - e^i_H$$

$$u^i_L = \alpha\left[\pi^i_{HL}\mu^i + \pi^i_{LL}(1-\mu^i)\right] + \beta\left[(1-\pi^i_{HL})\mu^i + (1-\pi^i_{LL})(1-\mu^i)\right] - e^i_L \tag{6}$$

where we subtract the cost of effort. The present values of payoffs are,

$$V_H^O = u_H^O/\delta, \qquad V_L^O = u_L^O/\delta,$$

$$V_H^I = u_H^O/\delta + (u_H^I - u_H^O)/(\delta + \eta_H), \qquad V_L^I = u_L^O/\delta + (u_L^I - u_L^O)/(\delta + \eta_L), \tag{7}$$

Outsiders, in the first row of equation (7), simply get instantaneous utility discounted at rate δ. Insiders (second row) get additional utility for as long as they stay in the group. Under our assumptions (and with effort levels and group entry probabilities the same for all individuals) the instantaneous gains to being in the group are the same for high and low ability individuals, so $u_H^I - u_H^O = u_L^I - u_L^O$. However, the present value of being in the in-group is greater for high ability than low ability individuals, $V_H^I - V_H^O > V_L^I - V_L^O$. The reason is simply that they expect the benefits of group membership to last longer, as they are less likely to be involved in a failing project and to be ejected ($\eta_L > \eta_H$).

This result drives several amplification effects. Suppose that individuals choose the level of effort they put in to maximize present value payoffs (equation (7)). An increase in effort increases the probability of success, and this is particularly valuable for insiders as it reduces the probability of ejection (equations (2)). First order conditions give, for outsiders and insiders respectively,

$$(\alpha - \beta)f'(e_j^O) = 1, \qquad j = H, L$$

$$[\alpha - \beta + \gamma(V_j^I - V_j^O)]f'(e_j^I) = 1, \qquad j = H, L \tag{8}$$

We see that insiders work harder than outsiders because they fear ejection from the group. This effort effect is greater for more able people because $V_H^I - V_H^O > V_L^I - V_L^O$, so has the effect of further refining the group – high ability people work harder, are more likely to succeed, and hence have a still higher probability of staying in the group.

Finally, what proportion of new entrants to the labor force initially enter the in-group or not – how are λ_H and λ_L determined? We assume that all individuals can enter the group, but now add a cost to entry – perhaps the cost of working in a more expensive city, or of time invested in building initial contacts with the group. We model this as a fixed cost c that varies across individuals. Indexing members of the population by z, the cost takes the form, $c = \bar{c} + \tilde{c}z$, $z \in [0,1]$. The proportions of high and low ability individuals who initially enter the in-group are obtained by finding the marginal entrant for whom the fixed cost equals the expected premium to being in the group, so:

$$\lambda_H = \left|V_H^I - V_H^O - \bar{c}\right|/\tilde{c}, \qquad \lambda_L = \left|V_L^I - V_L^O - \bar{c}\right|/\tilde{c} \tag{9}$$

Once again, we see that the inequality $V_H^I - V_H^O > V_L^I - V_L^O$ causes a higher proportion of high ability than of low ability to enter the group initially. Entry costs therefore act as a self-selection mechanism, further increasing the ability gap between insiders and outsiders.

The results that we have outlined can be usefully summarized by a numerical example, given in table 2. The first column is the base case. Using parameters given in the appendix and an ejection probability of 0.8%, the 'in-group' accounts for 18.4% of the population. It contains a substantially higher proportion of able people than the population at large, and yields its members higher present value utility than is received by outsiders. This effect is greater for high than for low ability individuals, $V_H^I - V_H^O > V_L^I - V_L^O$. Remaining columns allow for endogenous choice of effort and costs of entry to the group. If effort is endogenous people in the group work harder than outsiders and, since $V_H^I - V_H^O > V_L^I - V_L^O$, high ability group members put in more effort than low ability ones. The effect is to increase group size as failure probabilities are reduced, and to increase the proportion of the in-group that is high ability, μ^I. Column 3 gives the effect of a cost of entering the group. Although this cost is the same for high and low ability people the return to being in the group is greater for high ability people. Thus, in this example, 81% of high ability people enter, compared to just 25% of low ability. The final column gives outcomes with endogenous effort and entry costs. This case compounds the previous effects, giving the highest value of μ^I, the proportion of the in-group that is high ability.

	BASE	EFFORT	COSTS OF ENTRY	EFFORT AND ENTRY COSTS
φ	0.184	0.203	0.132	0.224
μ^I	0.496	0.514	0.797	0.799
μ^O	0.293	0.283	0.258	0.194
V_H^I	6.07	6.41	6.62	7.19
V_L^I	1.44	1.73	1.56	1.7
V_H^O	5.82	6.07	5.66	5.67
V_L^O	1.32	1.57	1.16	1.17
λ_H	1	1	0.81	1
λ_L	1	1	0.25	0.37

Table 2 Group formation: $\gamma = 0.8$.

Who are the gainers and who are the losers from this process? Rows 4-7 give the present value of individuals' utilities.[43] If no group existed, all high ability individuals would have the same utility, as would all low ability individuals. Existence of the group creates a gap between insiders and outsiders, and this gap is larger for high-ability individuals than low ability, and is greater when effort is endogenous and entry costs cause selection of individuals initially entering the group. Outsiders are the big losers as refinement of group membership forces them to make worse matches. The gainers from the in-group are the high ability insiders. However, it is interesting to note that even these individuals do not want failure of a project to lead to ejection with probability 1. Varying γ, it turns out that their utility is typically maximised at some value between zero and unity. Too low, and the group is not of high enough average quality; too high, and even high ability insiders face a significant probability of ejection.

This brings us back to our central points. F2F contact removes anonymity and allows people to judge and be judged. If you have been observed to fail then – with probability γ – you are branded an outsider, and group members will no longer seek to match with you. The magnitude of γ is, in many activities, inherently spatial. In a faceless and anonymous world $\gamma = 0$, and in-groups cannot form. F2F contact raises γ, creating the possibility of group formation. By removing anonymity F2F raises the probability of good, step-by-step iterative judgements about the abilities of others. An in-group that forms to generate and share this information improves the quality of matches made by workers, and also sharpens the incentives for individuals to succeed and increases the work effort of group members.

4. F2F, buzz and the coordination of economic activities

4.1 Buzz cities

Previous sections have highlighted the key features of F2F contact. It is a highly efficient technology of communication; a means of overcoming coordination and incentive problems in uncertain environments; a key element of the socialization that in turn allows people to be candidates for membership of 'in-groups' and to stay in such groups; and a direct source of psychological motivation. The combined effects of these features we term 'buzz'. We speculate that there is a superadditivity in these effects, generating increasing returns for the people and the activities involved. Individuals in a buzz environment interact and cooperate with other high-ability people, are well placed to communicate complex ideas with them, and are highly motivated. To be able to reap these benefits in full almost invariably requires co-

---

[43] Where entry costs are incurred values are reported for the median individual in the group.

location, rather than occasional interludes of F2F contact. It is unsurprising that people in a buzz environment should be highly productive.

Amongst examples of this sort of interaction are joint projects in science, engineering and research. A large literature demonstrates the existence of localized, industry-specific knowledge spillovers within the science- and technology-based industries.[44] Networks of firms and industries clustered within regions interact more heavily with co-located university-based scientists than with those in other regions.[45] This is associated with higher rates of commercialization than at long distances. Moreover, the various benefits of F2F that are established through long periods of colocation are durable: they have been shown to manifest themselves amongst people who then move away but continue to work together, and are much stronger than the contacts between long-distance partners.[46]

In many buzz cities there is also cross-fertilization between sectorally-specialized networks. High technology and government have close interactions, for example, and this is why Washington DC has become a major high-technology region. Design and entertainment/ communications have strong crossover effects in their development of content, and this is why places such as NY, LA, London and Paris concentrate them together.[47] Higher education, finance and government are a powerful nexus of ideas and contact networks for the socialization of elites and the coordination of their joint projects. These various inter-network, highly dynamic and unplanned contact systems were alluded to by Jacobs, in her intuition that urban diversity is central to certain kinds of economic creativity because of the specific advantages of unplanned and haphazard, inter-network contact.[48] Co-location is especially important to these processes because it provides a low-cost way for new ideas and talent to make their way into existing activities, by facilitating access for newcomers and by lowering the costs of evaluation on the part of those already in the relevant loops. New relationships are hence made easier, cheaper and much more effective than they would be without co-location.

---

[44] Zoltan J. Acz, *Innovation and the growth of cities* (Cheltenham: Edward Elgar, 2002).

[45] Michael R. Darby and Lynne G. Zucker, 'Growing by leaps and inches: creative destruction, real cost reduction, and inching up' (Cambridge, MA: NBER Working Paper No. w8947, May 2002) www.nber.org/papers/w8947.

[46] Stefano Breschi and Francesco Lissoni, 'Mobility and social networks: localised knowledge spillovers revisited' (Milan: University Bocconi, CESPRI Working Paper No. 142, 2003).

[47] Andy C. Pratt, 'Firm boundaries? The organization of new media production in SF 1996-98' (London: LSE Dept of Geography, manuscript, 2002); Allen J Scott, *On Hollywood* (Princeton, NJ: Princeton University Press, 2004, in press).

[48] Jacobs, The economy of cities *op. cit.*

In diversified city economies, functional agglomerations consist of pieces of different sectors sharing common input structures and common clients.[49] Buzz cities, we suggest, derive their agglomerative force both from the classical network agglomeration efficiencies and from the inter-network, interactive knowledge and information-based activities including: (a) creative and cultural functions (including industries linked to this, such as fashion, design and the arts); (b) finance and business services; (c) science, technology and high technology and research;[50] and (d) power and influence (government, headquarters, trade associations, and international agencies).[51] These cities' attraction for talent and their efficiency in socializing individuals confer important advantages on their participants. Buzz cities continue to have such force today because they are the places where, more than ever, critical problems of coordination in the modern economy are resolved through F2F contact.

Paradoxically, buzz cities are often those we most closely associate with globalization, because they are important nodes of highly developed international business and culture networks, with high levels of international travel-and-meeting activity, and high concentrations of both high-skilled and low-skilled immigrants. They often host many multinational enterprises. The most globalized cities also seem to have the most localized buzz. This is not surprising in view of the analysis provided here. The highest levels of international business require insertion into locally-grounded government and political networks in order to function efficiently.

4.2 Buzz and alternative modes of coordination

Buzz is an important, or even essential, part of the way in which some activities operate, while for other activities it is unimportant. Table 3 offers a tentative taxonomy of alternative ways in which activities can be coordinated, in order to illustrate environments in which buzz is most important. The two dimensions by which activities are characterized are the kind of knowledge on which they are dependent, and the fluidity of the environment in which they operate.

In the right hand column are activities for which information is readily available/observable, such as production and trade in basic manufactures and commodities. Markets are the main mode through which such activities are coordinated. The

---

[49] Gilles Duranton and Diego Puga, 'From sectoral to functional urban specialisation' (CEPR Discussion Paper No. 2971, 2001).

[50] Though, as Florida points out, there is a detailed geography of creative workers within metropolitan areas. People in the fashion, design, government and finance sectors tend to inhabit different parts of the metropolitan space from those in science and engineering; Florida, The rise of the creative class *op. cit.*

[51] Hall, Cities in civilization *op. cit.*; Scott, Global city regions *op. cit.*

knowledge requirement of such activities is not a force for clustering – the proximity requirement is low.

Other activities are more dependent on specialist or private information, sometimes codified, and sometimes tacit. The middle column gives cases where the information can be codified, e.g. in well-defined engineering or chemical blueprints. Such activities are frequently internalized within firms or bureaucracies. The reasons for this have been extensively analyzed in the literature on the boundaries of the firm.[52] For example, intangible assets such as proprietary knowledge, reputation or good-will can be dissipated if traded through arms length transactions between firms. Internalization within an organization does not necessarily imply a high spatial proximity requirement.

	KNOWLEDGE USED IN COORDINATION		
ENVIRONMENT OF COORDINATION	SPECIALISED/ PRIVATE		UBIQUITOUS/ TRANSPARENT
	TACIT	CODIFIED	
STABLE	Bureaucracy/ firms Specialised networks for search/ matching (*HIGH*) **Financial services**	Bureaucracy/ firms (*LOW*) **Car industry (mass production)**	Markets (*LOW*) **Basic manufactured inputs or services**
FLUID	Buzz (*HIGH*) **Culture, politics, arts, academia, new technologies, advanced finance**	Organized networks for search/ matching (*MEDIUM*) **Aerospace, pharmaceuticals**	Markets (*LOW*) **Commodities (e.g. oil)**

Table 3 Modes of coordination (Proximity requirement in italics)

Where information is largely codified but the environment is subject to significant fluctuation there may also be organized networks to facilitate search and matching of partners. This may create pressures for agglomeration due to the transactions costs associated with managing the input-output relations designed to cope with fluctuations in the environment. F2F contact is likely to be an important element of coordination, of both the market and contractual relations in the organized project

---

[52] Bengt Holmström and John Roberts, 'The boundaries of the firm revisited', *Journal of Economic Perspectives* 12, 4 (1998) pp. 73-94.

system at hand. But the nature of F2F contact in this case is fundamentally different from the F2F which is used in finding partners. Instead, such F2F is about monitoring the project organization, where the partners and the purposes of the collaboration (its intended outputs) are already defined. Such monitoring may require the rapid-fire interaction and parallel processing of F2F, but it rarely involves the incentive problems of joint project formation or the complex processes of getting into loops which are associated with co-location. Under some circumstances it can therefore be carried out through occasional long-distance travel. Large-scale technology development projects, as in the aerospace or pharmaceuticals industries, are an example of this use of F2F without co-location.

The left-hand column gives cases where knowledge is tacit and is typically embodied in highly skilled workers. The need to communicate this knowledge creates a high proximity requirement. All this is amplified if the knowledge is fluid or the environment uncertain, as in the bottom left hand corner. This is the environment where buzz comes to the fore, because the uncertainty concerns not only the content of relevant information, but the purposes to which it will be put and the people who will be involved in using it.

5. The future of F2F contact and colocation

The emphasis on F2F might seem paradoxical to some, since the advent of broadband internet communications would appear, finally, to provide us the means to avoid F2F contact. The internet has enabled certain kinds of complex communication to occur at a distance which were previously constrained by proximity, and some have gone so far as to claim that this is leading to the "death of distance".[53]

The reality is certainly more complicated than this, however. The history of economic geography suggests a continuing tension between two opposing forces. On the one hand, there is ongoing transformation of complex and unfamiliar coordination tasks into routine activities that can be successfully accomplished at remote but cheaper locations. This is reflected in the codification of information, stabilization of meanings, and the reduction of incentive problems (opening up the possibility of more complete contracting), so that less F2F contact is needed. Its principal geographical consequence is the tendency towards deagglomeration or dispersion of production. On the other hand, bursts of innovations create new activities which can only initially be carried out via complex and unfamiliar coordination tasks. At any given moment, these two opposing forces combine in

---

[53] Frances Cairncross, *The death of distance: how the communications revolution is changing our lives* (Boston, MA: Harvard Business School Press, 2001).

different ways, according to the activity at hand. The borderline between those activities which are amenable to relocation at a distance due to reduction in the cost and complexity of their associated transactions, and the new complex activities which require F2F and other forms of geographical proximity, is in constant evolution. New technologies may facilitate dispersion of production, but they also destabilize activities, creating uncertainty, research questions, and unknown opportunities. This is an environment in which information is rapidly changing and knowledge is tacit, conducive to buzz. It leads to a prediction that though the precise mix of activities involving F2F and co-location will change, they will constitute an important set of such activities well into the future, and will continue to generate agglomeration of highly-skilled individuals, firms, and bureaucracies in high-cost urban centers.

Appendix 1

Payoffs are expected monetary gains minus e_i. A good project sends out signal that it is good with probability γ, and a false signal with probability $1 - \gamma$. A bad project sends out a false signal (that it is good) with probability β_i, and the true signal with probability $1 - \beta_i$, where $\beta_i = (\gamma^2 + e_i)^{-0.5}$. Thus, if no effort is expended, $\beta_i = \gamma$.
Parameter values: $A = 150$, $C = 50$, $\varrho = 1/3$, $\gamma = 0.8$.
Probabilities are all computed by Bayes theorem and figure 1 is computed in GAUSS.

Appendix 2

Parameter values: $\bar{\mu} = 0.33$, $* = 0.1$, $\forall = 1$, $\exists = 0$, $(= 0.8$, $\Delta_{HH} = 0.9$, $\Delta_{HL} = 0.45$, $\Delta_{LL} = 0$, $\bar{c} = 0.15$, $\tilde{c} = 1$. Effort function: $f(e) = se^{0.5}$, $s = 0.2$.

TECHNOLOGY, ORGANIZATION,
TERRITORY

Technology, organization, territory: a biographical interview with Michael Storper*

MICHAEL HOYLER, TIM FREYTAG and HEIKE JÖNS

Berkeley

You received your academic degrees at the University of California at Berkeley in the late 1970s and early 1980s. How did this period and place influence your work and your approach to economic geography?

The relationship was quite strong. I was a half generation too late for the revolution of the 60s and early 70s, but from a very young age I had been attracted by all the radical things that were happening at the period. So when I was thirteen or fourteen years old, I was involved in demonstrations against the Vietnam war, hanging out with people older than me. That's probably one of the reasons why I went to Berkeley. Things had happened at other universities, but Berkeley was the epicentre of all this action and it had the additional attraction of being linked to San Francisco, the epicentre of 'counter-culture'.

I started out studying history and sociology. To be honest, what I was really interested in was political activism. I was involved in the environmental movement at the same time as I was studying. I took some classes that made me think about long-term economic social development as a structured process. I can remember the German sociologist Reinhard Bendix distinctly, who wrote classical books about the

---

* The following interview was conducted during the 7th Hettner Lectures at the University of Heidelberg, given by Michael Storper in June 2003. It aims to retrace the making of Storper's relational economic geography by exploring links between biography, academic networks and knowledge production (for recent theoretically informed enquiries into 'geographical biographies', see Trevor J. Barnes, 'Lives lived and lives told: biographies of geography's quantitative revolution', *Environment and Planning D: Society and Space* 19 (2001) pp. 409-29; David N. Livingstone, 'Knowledge, space and the geographies of science', in his *Science, space and hermeneutics* (Heidelberg: Department of Geography, 2002) pp. 7-40). Secondly, we aim to contribute to ongoing debates about Storper's conceptual arguments, not least in German-speaking economic geography, where his concept of a 'holy trinity' has recently been key to the call for a paradigmatic change in the discipline (see Harald Bathelt and Johannes Glückler, *Wirtschaftsgeographie: ökonomische Beziehungen in räumlicher Perspektive* (Stuttgart: Ulmer, 2002)). Finally, we hope that the interview's emphasis on the social construction of economic knowledge will encourage critical engagement not only with Storper's arguments but with one's own positionality within the vibrant field of economic geography.

This interview was first published in *Zeitschrift für Wirtschaftsgeographie (The German Journal of Economic Geography)* 48 (1) (2004) pp. 63-72 and is reprinted here with the permission of the editors.

structure of industrial society. The other was a young instructor, Ann Swidler, who taught classes about 'the very long run', a course about the history of family life from 1400 to the 20th century. Those two classes made me realize that the world is structured by institutions. But I was also very interested in economics. This was the time when the old economy was breaking down and the core regions of the country, in the north-east, were losing their employment, the industries were shutting down, they were moving to the south or to other countries. All these things were really fascinating to me.

Towards the end of my undergraduate career I had to decide what to do. The logical thing for me was to do a doctorate in sociology. So I applied to different sociology departments, but sociology was a strange discipline at that time. It was torn apart by disputes between 'new radicals', Marxists and others, and the 'old schools' of structural functionalism. To a young person looking at the field, it was frightening to see all of your professors fighting with each other. Then I thought about becoming an economist, in particular because at Berkeley there were a few young radical economists teaching about labour economics. The economy really interested me but, once I started going beyond the radicals' courses, I realized what economics was likely to be like, which is, the maths was very difficult, the paradigms were very strict. It was attractive in a scientific way, but I felt that I was probably never going to be good enough at the mathematical modelling part to be a really good economist in the standard sense of it. I struggled through it and learned how to do that stuff, but felt in the heart that I wasn't interested enough to put in the effort to be good.

I had a kind of a personal crisis, I thought, what am I going to do with my life? I floundered around, and got more deeply involved in environmental activism. After a number of campaigns in which I was a kind of voluntary citizen, militant type, I got employed in the environmental group 'Friends of the Earth', who had its headquarters in San Francisco. I started learning how to write reports, to analyze things, flying back and forth to Washington, giving testimony, all the aspects of political lobbying in America. In a way I laugh at it because I was way too young to do it. I really enjoyed it and learned how to function in a political world a bit, but after a while I wanted to go back and become an academic. I still didn't know how I was going to do this, go into economics, go into sociology…

Right at that time some friend of mine said, 'There is this young assistant professor in geography, Dick Walker, and you should go and talk to him'. I had never taken a class in geography, it didn't mean anything to me. So I went over and talked to this young guy who had just arrived from the east coast, where he had been a student of David Harvey. Everything that I was interested in, he was interested in. He said to me 'Why don't you apply to the geography department?' And that's how it happened. I started out working on environmental questions, but very quickly turned to questions of economic geography, the shifting locations of industry, the redrawing of the map of the economy.

When you started your PhD in the geography department, you had not been influenced by any geographical thinking before – you drew your intellectual inspirations from history, sociology and economics. How did you experience this change in your academic affiliation?

When I came into geography there were, in the Berkeley faculty, a lot of people who were interested in what we would call 'geographical thought'. I can remember this funny moment when I had to defend my dissertation proposal and the committee got together. Dick Walker was my chair and I worked pretty closely with Allan Pred, and there was Ann Markusen and Manuel Castells who both taught in the city planning department and there was this geographer's geographer named David Hooson. And he said to me, 'Tell me, what does this have to do with geography?' Well, more elegantly, he wanted me to show how it related to geographical thought. To be honest, I had a weak culture in geographical thought and I still don't have all that strong a culture in what people would call the classics of geographical thought. My culture is a lot stronger in classics of sociology and even economics and I think it probably shows up in my work today. I'm really a social scientist. Geography has its feet in a lot of different places, in social science, in history, in philosophy, and in the physical sciences. And these other parts are relatively foreign to me. In the geography department at Berkeley there were all kinds of different intellectual cultures interacting and it took me a long time to understand all that was going on. In addition, I had unusually strong relationships to this big group of students who were studying regional economic development in the city planning department with Manuel Castells, Peter Hall, Ann Markusen and a few other people. That was very formative to me, because I had always been between and at the edge of different disciplines.

Marxism

This was the time when Marxism was strong, when structuralism was very strong. To what degree did you subscribe to a Marxist approach in your early research?

I was hardcore Marxist to begin with. Dick Walker, David Harvey's star PhD student, was known as 'the new Marxist on campus'. He taught classes with a very strong Marxist perspective, and in addition gave classes on how to read Marx's *Capital* in a place called the 'East Bay Socialist School'. There was also Manuel Castells, Marxist at that time, Ann Markusen, young leader of what is called the 'Union for Radical Political Economics'. There was a young economics professor called Michael Reich, doing Marxist economics of labour. A number of us were trying to expand what

David Harvey had begun in his book *Social justice and the city*[1], and to push it forward into a kind of full-fledged model of, in my case, an economic geography. The first article that Dick Walker and I wrote together in 1981 was called "Capital and industrial location"[2]. While I was still a student, we were beginning to outline ideas that would find themselves later in our book *The capitalist imperative*[3]. It was an attempt to see the process of spatial development in the same structured way that Marxists saw the rest of the economy.

When did you start to explore alternative paths, divert from the pure Marxist way?

Very early on, actually. Dick Walker taught me the big picture about how Marxism would view capitalism. Marxism says capitalists exploit workers, fair enough, but when you start to look at specifics, a particular industry undergoing organizational and locational change – what are the precise mechanisms and processes? In the early years, what I was trying to do, was fill in missing layers in the Marxist analysis. I was trying to give it what I would call 'technological realism'. In my doctoral research, I took four industries that were undergoing big change. Three of them were old industries, steel, textiles and automobiles, and one of them was a new industry, microelectronics, semiconductors. And I wanted to see how and why they were relocating, and how they chose their relocations. In the middle of studying all of that, I came to realize that a whole new economy was in the making. If you were trained in Marxist radicalism in those days, you read Harry Braverman's *Labour and monopoly capital*[4] in which he told the story that capitalists use technology to take the skills away from workers: The purpose of technological change is to streamline and routinize labour processes, so that labourers lose their skills, and their wages are reduced. And that's of course part of the process in a lot of industries. Even the non-Marxist sociologists who had studied post-war modernization told this story. But no one had yet analyzed a complete cycle of creation of new industries and new sectors.

Right in the middle of all that a number of us started to see the beginnings of Silicon Valley in the San Francisco Bay area. For example, one of my fellow students, AnnaLee Saxenian, wrote the first academic paper on Silicon Valley.[5] She

---

[1] David Harvey, *Social justice and the city* (Baltimore: Johns Hopkins University Press, 1973).

[2] Richard Walker and Michael Storper, 'Capital and industrial location', *Progress in Human Geography* 5 (1981) pp. 473-509.

[3] Richard Walker and Michael Storper, *The capitalist imperative: territory, technology, and industrial growth* (Oxford: Blackwell, 1989).

[4] Harry Braverman, *Labour and monopoly capital: the degradation of work in the twentieth century* (New York, London: Monthly Review Press, 1974).

[5] AnnaLee Saxenian, 'The urban contradictions of Silicon Valley: regional growth and the restructuring of the semiconductor industry', *International Journal of Urban and Regional Research* 7 (1983) pp. 237-61.

subsequently went away to MIT to do her doctoral thesis, but we started out together. We were a group of people who used to go on weekends to this funny place, where there was this new electronics industry and ask, 'What's going on? This is weird, what is all this about?' The reality started to explode in my face. I began to think that somehow, even though Marxism had a lot of good lessons, it just seemed really incomplete. For one thing, it didn't seem to get the story about innovation very well. Marxism is obsessed with the notion of "crisis" in capitalism, and though Marx himself suggested that crises can precede innovation, most Marxists are really just interested in how such crises lead either to the downfall of capitalism or to negative consequences for the working class. The latter is, of course an interesting issue, but the former is not. Still, at that time, I wasn't actually ready to make a clean break with Marxism. It would take me a long time to actually figure out that in the end, though Marxism calls our attention to the deep distributional conflicts in capitalism and to its incessant dynamic of change, most such issues can be better analyzed with other theories and approaches, and that Marxism's political analyses are largely irrelevant.

Los Angeles

After finishing your degree in Berkeley, you went to UCLA. Your work started to focus on Hollywood's film industry and the nature of industrial clusters. How did this change come about and how did your work relate to what is often referred to as the 'California School'?

When I went down to UCLA, I got hired into the city planning department originally, and who became my colleague? Ed Soja, a geographer. But also other people who were not geographers, one of the major figures of thinking about cities, John Friedmann, an Austrian who went to the United States, and Dolores Hayden, a famous feminist student of cities. One year before I came to UCLA, Allen Scott had arrived from Toronto. He was already beginning to think about the southern California economy, about industrial systems and new forms of industrialization, as were the Berkeley group because of Silicon Valley. So, another interesting collection of people was forming in Los Angeles.

I got to Los Angeles and, as a good geographer, said to myself, 'I should figure out a new research project and do something here in the region.' At the time the newspapers in LA were filled with stories about the crisis of Hollywood and how Hollywood was leaving, going to other places to shoot films. This reminded me of issues I dealt with in my dissertation. Along with one of my fellow graduate students from Berkeley who had come to LA also to work at that time, Susan Christopherson, we decided to study the film industry. We asked why and how Hollywood was undergoing reorganization and leaving southern California. However, in the middle of our project we discovered that Hollywood was not leaving Hollywood. It was staying, but it was reorganizing and a whole new model of production organization was coming about, which is what we would call today 'flexible specialization'. In the 1920s, 30s and 40s there had been big firms in Hollywood, but starting in the 50s and going through the 60s, 70s and 80s, these big firms had largely externalized their production to small firms and now there was a project by project system of production organization, which actually reinforced the agglomeration economies of Hollywood. The average firm size in Hollywood had declined. We began to tell a story about an industrial cluster, and in so doing discovered the subject.

Right in the middle of this work, Michael Piore and Charles Sabel published *The second industrial divide*[6]. They had worked a lot on industrial districts in the 'Third Italy', made a general theory out of it and made it known to English speaking audiences. It was a big important book. The notion that we had gone from a mass production economy into a flexibly organized network economy. 1984, that's when Susan and I are coming up with our interpretation of what's going on in Hollywood, when AnnaLee Saxenian is working on Silicon Valley, when Allen Scott is working on the electronics components industry and the clothing industry in southern California. Through the work of Piore and Sabel we learned that there were all these people who had written about the phenomenon of small firm clusters in Italy. So we started to read them, for example the classical book on Italy by Arnaldo Bagnasco, *The three Italies*[7]. Then of course the Florentine school led by Giacomo Becattini. All of a sudden there is this shape of a new world coming about. Until then what people really thought about were big industries and mass production. Clusters, small firms and networks just didn't exist as a thought paradigm. It wasn't what we were taught to look for. It started to congeal at this moment, both empirically and theoretically.

The 'California School' – I don't know if it really is a school – was only part of a movement that was popping up in different places. There was the Piore and Sabel branch, which was MIT-centered, there was what was going on in Italy, and later there was a smattering of Germans trying to deal with places like Baden-Württemberg, and a few Danes… The image of the new realities started to emerge and then communication started to happen between the different places where people were thinking about their own realities. The California School was in part a reaction to that. That's what became for me a second wave of theoretical work, where Allen Scott and I tried to think about the theory of agglomeration. We tried to draw on the classical works about the division of labour and scale and scope and how changes in that might produce changes in the linkages of firms and hence the

---

[6] Michael J. Piore and Charles F. Sabel, *The second industrial divide: possibilities for prosperity* (New York: Basic Books, 1984).

[7] Arnaldo Bagnasco, *Tre Italie: La problematica territoriale dello sviluppo italiano* (Bologna: Il Mulino, 1977).

geography of either clustering or spreading out. Once again, that was something that wasn't necessarily incompatible with Marxism but certainly wasn't part of Marxism.

The 'holy trinity': technology, organization and territory

In your book 'The regional world', published in 1997, you come up with the concept of a 'holy trinity' in which you link technology, organization and territory to explain regional differences in economic development. How did you arrive at this heterodox approach?

To understand where this came from I need to add a couple of more biographical elements. Already in the book that Dick Walker and I did in the late 1980s there was a kind of hybrid thing going on. We were trying to deal with new, flexible forms of industrialization by coming up with notions of technological and organizational change that were behind the 'capitalist imperative'. After this first phase of working on theories of agglomeration and the division of labour I wanted to have a more systematic understanding of technological and organizational change, of those forces that would lead to agglomeration or dispersion of industry. I began to interact more with economists and organization theorists. Around that time there were two really interesting things happening. One was that some economists were starting to talk about what is now known as *evolutionary processes* of technological change. They were also talking about these processes as somehow *institutionally* structured. They began to come up with the notion that technological change is highly structured by institutions and that these institutions tend to differ from place to place. What we now call national systems of innovation – why, say, is Germany developing some technologies and going in one direction and the United States is developing other technologies and going in a different direction? There were random factors, but what we actually end up using or implementing gets selected by the institutions that are there to make choices at certain points. There are then distinctive evolutionary pathways of technology. They are not necessarily optimal or defined by any perfect efficiency criterion. This was a major thing happening in the late 80s and early 90s and I started to be interested in this because of my research in comparative industrial agglomeration.

I should also say that being involved in studies of agglomerations and local industrial systems, both Allen Scott and I had begun to make regular trips to Italy where we were interacting with the 'Third Italy' group. And we had started interacting with the MIT group. I know there were things we were learning about Baden-Württemberg at the time too, the people were starting to filter into the English language literature. For one thing, Gary Herrigel had studied with Charles Sabel and was writing for 'Anglo-Saxons' about Germany and then people like Wolfgang Streek and a few others, I can remember papers coming out of the Wissenschaftszentrum in Berlin. So, when you start interacting, two things happen to you intellectually. You begin to see the commonalities, but you also start to see differences.

For me the question of difference and specificity in these forms of new industrial development began to be interesting. I applied for a grant in the late 80s from the German Marshall Fund of the United States. What I proposed to do was a three country comparative study of industrial districts: United States, France and Italy. The real reason that France was in there was because I spoke French. We had had more interaction with the Italians, but I spoke French and thought I might as well play to my talents, so I based myself in Paris. That's where the European branch of the story started. It was absolutely not planned to become Euro-American, which is in fact what has happened to me. There is obviously a personal history side of it, falling in love, the other thing was building networks of colleagues and intellectual networks and getting invited back, ultimately leading to a kind of institutionalization. I ended up being equally influenced by what was going on in the English-language world and by what was happening in certain parts of Europe.

In that year funded by the German Marshall Fund I started out comparing different institutional forms of industrial districts. It was really difficult to come up with a theory. For example, I was comparing the furniture industry in the United States and in the 'Third Italy'. I thought, ok, I can describe this. In America, we make furniture in large numbers, mass production. In Italy they make mostly design, high quality furniture. What really struck me in trying to do this comparative work was that the ways that people relate to each other are different. That seems very basic, but in trying to study this question I met some French colleagues who were working on what they called *conventions*. Ultimately institutions exist in our lives because we incorporate them in our individual actions. They came up with the notion that the way they are incorporated in our individual actions are through conventions, which are something like principles of mutual expectations by which we relate to each other. And these differ from industry to industry and from place to place.

I thought that this would be an interesting way to explain why the Italians organize their furniture industry as a high quality design-oriented industry based on face-to-face interpersonal contact, while the Americans apply principles of mass production to theirs. In the actual daily life of doing this, there are different conventions at work. Robert Salais and I came up with the idea that basically these were like systems of action, which we called 'worlds' or 'worlds of production'. So, we did a book together on the subject, which came out in 1993 in French as *Les mondes de production* and then in 1997 in English.[8] Behind all that, I was seeing the geography issue and I began to

---

[8] Robert Salais and Michael Storper, *Les mondes de production: enquête sur l'identité économique de la France* (Paris: Éditions de l'École des hautes études en sciences sociales, 1993); Michael Storper and Robert Salais, *Worlds of production: the action frameworks of the economy* (Cambridge, MA: Harvard University Press, 1997).

think that this was an interesting way into the comparative analysis of different regions. It was the notion that regions are different because the people in them are caught up in different systems of conventions, that is different systems of action and co-ordination of their actions.

Most economic geography had concentrated on linkages in the sense of 'linkages are basically processes of trade' – local trade in labour market or local trade in products, inputs and outputs. Remember, this is against a background of an empirical reality where there is less and less local trade in a lot of industries, there is long distance trade, cheapening transport and cheapening communication. I do not mean to say that local trade is never important. Obviously, when you look at industrial clusters in the Third Italy, it is. Local trade is important. But at that time, even in Silicon Valley, the system was maturing, there was a lot of long distance investment in Singapore and Malaysia, there were factories being opened up in the interior of the United States. So, what was going on in the local part of the system and why were these people clustering together? From the work on conventions, I began to think, maybe what these people share is not that they are shipping products back and forth across the street, it's that somehow they are co-ordinated by shared systems of action. This is what I tried to capture in the term *untraded interdependencies*. These seemed to matter more in some cases than the traded linkages.

And this is where the threads come together ...

Yes, that led me to the *holy trinity*. I'd been really steeped in all this work about technological change and evolutionary economics. All those people were talking about 'technological spillovers'. They were on to this mystery of technological change which is both an individual and a collective process. From what I was thinking about action systems and their geography, of people being close together because of sharing principles that enable them to co-ordinate with each other, it was a short leap to saying that maybe what actually enables people to bring about these technological spillovers in localized space, is that they have untraded interdependencies between each other. That was step number one: *technologies* in the holy trinity.

Then, step number two was firms. The most important form of *organization* in capitalism is the firm. The economy is like a big puzzle of overlapping organizational levels. There's the sectoral level, the firm level, the industrial system level, the technological field level, the regional level, the national level ... for me it's like an organizational puzzle. It seemed to me that fundamentally to understand the geography of the economy, you had to understand the construction, deconstruction and reconstruction of its organizational forms. If you look at an economy in a dynamic perspective, what you have are production systems that mutate – sometimes into a big firm, sometimes into a fragmented production system, sometimes into combinations of these. That's driven by technologies largely. The technologies drive economies of scale and scope and transaction costs and that makes organizational systems mutate into different forms. But firms exist partly because of shared action systems among people that tie them together and make firms or production systems work the way they do. That had to be the second element of a holy trinity.

And then of course, because of all the work on agglomeration, there was *territory*. As a geographer, I had been able to see that technologies have a big impact on driving these organizational mutations. And these organizational mutations in turn create needs for co-ordination among the different units that are the results of those processes. And the co-ordinations of those linkages have a geography. But it's not just that. Geography is not just an outcome but also a cause – now here is where I really do have a geographer's culture. Once you've studied places, you know that the people in the places have shared conventions that enable them to co-ordinate. It's an additional level of co-ordination of modern economic and social life, that has its own existence in addition to all the other levels that we know about, like sectors and firms. And therefore geography actually could have feedback effects on how production systems are organized and even on what kinds of technologies are produced because the ability of people to co-ordinate together would have an effect on what kinds of technological synergies they could have.

Three subdivisions, but each of them having dynamic feedbacks on the other. And each of them being co-ordinated in hard ways through hard linkages and traded processes, but also in soft ways through untraded interdependencies.

What inspired you to use a religious metaphor – holy trinity – for the three key elements of your concept?

I was writing a paper for an Italian conference. There is this colloquium every two years in Tuscany, which is organized by Professor Becattini's group in Florence. It's called the 'Incontri pratesi sullo sviluppo locale' and is held in the Villa Medicea di Artimino. I had been invited to this meeting before, but in 1996 they invited me to give the opening speech in the town hall of Prato. I had to do it in Italian, so I had to find some way to overcome the fact that my Italian is really terrible. I thought, 'well, I've got a triangle of things' – this goes to show you how really silly these things are – 'it's a catholic country, what's three things? It's the holy trinity!'. I called up an Italian friend and asked, 'how do you say holy trinity in Italian?' And so she said to me *Santissima Trinità*. I wrote the speech and faxed it to her and she corrected all the Italian, and I got up there in the town hall of Prato and said – it was the first time I had ever gone public with this – I want to propose to you that the way you can see regional development is as a *holy trinity*. That's how it came about. Everyone laughed – I got their attention, that was the story.

Territorialization, embeddedness and relations

Your work has opened up the way for a relational perspective in economic geography that emphasizes the importance of social and institutional contexts for economic processes. In sociology, Mark Granovetter's concept of embeddedness has been similarly influential.[9] Do you see a link between your notion of territory and Granovetter's embeddedness?

I've always been very strongly admiring Mark Granovetter, who I think is a really brilliant sociologist. That's certainly something that inspired me as a geographer, that these industrial systems, these processes of technology development and change are not just sectorally determined, they're not just determined by non-geographical forces, something about places is making a distinctive contribution. The places are not just outcomes, they're causes. I've been struggling to make this point, to say that economic geography is not just about showing that the economy has a geography. That is, the economy expresses itself in geographical forms, but the geography makes the economy. Now, where is the problem with that? The problem is that as an assertion it doesn't mean anything. And it can't just be that the economy is spatially differentiated, therefore the geography makes the economy. You have to show that what happens in places has an influence on processes and forces that affect not only that place but other places.

Embeddedness is a good starting point. It suggests that certain forms of social actions are not transitive and contextless but somehow that the interaction context of these things matters. Still, as a geographer I felt that embeddedness needed to be pushed forward. There's a kind of residual analytical vagueness in the concept of embeddedness. In some senses the stuff I've been into more recently about information and knowledge and how understanding and communicating certain forms of knowledge depends not only on the knowledge itself but on the context in which it operates.

For me, the way to deal with context was the concept of *relations*, that somehow the action that a given economic agent can make depends on the interactions or the relational context of that action. Economics tells us about the sovereign actor, who, given a preference function and given some information, will make a choice. I'm of course inspired by the critique of that position, which is that in a lot of situations, we're not fully sovereign, we are actually interdependent to some degree, but then, what does interdependence mean? The way that I tried to give some substance to that was through the concept of relations. I see it as part of the project of articulating the notion of embeddedness.

---

[9] Mark Granovetter, 'Economic action and social structure: the problem of embeddedness', *American Journal of Sociology*, 91 (1985) pp. 481-510.

Cultural perspectives

More recently, the notion of a 'cultural turn' has entered Anglo-American economic geography. How do you relate to this widening of perspectives in the field?

This might sound strange coming from me, because many hardcore economic geographers or economists would probably see me as being very cultural. And yet I'm personally very uncomfortable with much of what is self-defined as the cultural turn in economic geography, actually the cultural turn in geography in general. I criticized it in a polemical article I wrote about this subject.[10] Behavioural, institutional, cultural, historical processes are of great importance to the way any economy develops. But the bottom line is, if you want to do good economic geography, you have to have economics. And economics is about analyzing causal processes that make markets work. I don't mean work in a necessarily positive way – it just enables us to get causes and effects. You can't dissolve the economics out of economic geography and still have economic geography.

The problem with certain people is that they want to describe the economy as one big cultural process. But it isn't. There are analytically describable forces in the economy. The laws of supply and demand have really big effects, whether it's in Heidelberg or in Toulouse or in Bamako. I'm against the notion that the cultural replaces the economic in economic geography. It may complement it, but it does not replace it.

What about the study of economic actors and their cultural practices, which can add an important dimension to understanding financial centres like the City of London, as, for example, Linda McDowell's work has shown?[11]

Of course there are many different and legitimate ways to study something like the City of London. It's a fantastically complex thing, it's an economic system, it's a system of social practices and interactions, it has cultural dimensions, it has symbolic dimensions, there are all kinds of social networks involved, it's representative in different ways, it's got organizations, it's got politics. So, sure, there is room for a lot of different things to be going on there.

It does seem to me though, that if you decide that what you are going to do is study the economic geography of, let's say, the advanced financial services industry, you cannot do that by merely calling attention to the cultures of the people involved. In other words, you can't say the economic geography of the advanced financial

---

[10] Michael Storper, 'The poverty of radical theory today: from the false promises of Marxism to the mirage of the cultural turn', *International Journal of Urban and Regional Research* 25 (2001) pp. 155-79.

[11] Linda McDowell, *Capital culture: gender at work in the city* (Oxford: Blackwell, 1997).

services sector in the world economy, of which the City of London is a major empirical manifestation, is explainable by the shared culture of financial managers, for example. For it to become an economic geography explanation, the story would have to be that the shared culture is the scarce resource, which the system economizes in the best way by concentrating the people who have this scarce resource in particular geographical areas. To tell an economic story, you have to, at some point, use economics.

There is another thing that is very bothersome to me about some of what I'm calling the 'cultural turn'. The historical weakness of geography as a discipline is its attraction to particularism and specificity, because of the belief that 'real places are specific and different'. The economists are the kings and queens of generality and universality, and we're the kings and queens of specificity and particularity. There is an atavistic impulse in a lot of geography, we've got to fly back to localism. In my view, the bad way to do that is to do old fashioned regional, ideographic geography. The good way to do it is to develop general theories that enable you to explain specific empirical processes. These can then be integrated into complex context-rich cases. This is different, however, from just doing descriptive regional geography.

Economic perspectives

Almost parallel with the cultural turn in geography, we could witness a spatial turn in economics, manifested in a so-called 'New Economic Geography'. [12] *How do you evaluate this development?*

The economists are doing good and bad at the same time. Let's start with the good part of their critique. Five or six years ago, I heard a talk by Paul Krugman. He made some points that hurt, but hit home. He said, 'I read a bunch of this regional science from the 50s, 60s and 70s, people like Walter Isard. A lot of what they were doing was interesting but because they didn't have a causal theory, they tried to deal with complexity by piling on layers.' So in the end you get a 'layer cake', which of course just collapses under its own weight, which is exactly what happened to regional science. The most unbelievably complex systems on systems on systems, really fancy statistical analysis, but pretty bad theory.

Modern differential calculus, plus general or partial equilibrium theory can enable you to cut through a lot of that and write simpler models than the regional scientist could do. And that's exactly what Krugman and the new economists did. They came along with better math, better computers and a good mastery of general and partial equilibrium theory and took all of these complex 'layer cake systems' and wrote what are relatively simple models that do better. And here is the horrible paradox – it's the

---

[12] E.g. Masahisa Fujita, Paul Krugman and Anthony J. Venables, *The spatial economy: cities, regions and international trade* (Cambridge, MA.: MIT Press, 1999).

geographers who should have been thinking not just about places as complex things that we have to describe densely. Places aren't just isolated, they are in constant relations to other places through factor mobility and trade, and hence each place's price formation and factor formation processes are caught up in relations of exchange and competition with other places. The New Economic Geography economists retheorized these relations in some very effective and innovative ways.

The bad part is that these economists don't have much of the sensitivity that we geographers, or sociologists or political scientists or students of technology have about real economies. They have simplifications that we find violent and unacceptable. Some of these economists are also very resistant to the soft side of things, the more complex behavioural patterns, relational issues and all that. Although economics of information is really into that now in very powerful ways. I'm very divided about it. In a lot of ways, these economists made a genuine new contribution, they put economics back into geography and geography back into economics. Our job though is to now accept the advances they've made, but to show them how to do it with greater geographical sensitivity. They are already at a risk of trivializing it into a new form of regional science. And that would be too bad, because the underlying questions they have opened up with their theoretical innovations are really interesting and important.

Challenges

We have talked about two poles in current thinking about economic geography. One is the new economists' version of a geographical economics, the other a cultural turn in economic geography itself. Where do you personally see the interesting and pressing theoretical questions for the field?

My dreamworld would be one where something like the holy trinity could be made more and more precise and operational. I really believe that there is this field of interlocking dynamics. And the problem is that each part of the holy trinity is in itself very complex, because the dynamics of technology, the dynamics of organizations, the dynamics of territories, each one in itself separately would be very difficult. Because each has a hard and a soft side and each has an evolutionary dynamic that also affects the evolutionary dynamic of the other. In fact, the reason that I proposed it was to show that the geographical dynamics are not just outcomes but causes of the economy and its structures. Here is where I have always felt that geography was never given its fair recognition. You ask an economist, is technology important to the evolutionary of the economy, and they'll say yes. You ask an economist, are institutions important to the evolution of the economy, and they'll say yes. You ask an economist, is politics important to the evolution of the economy, and they'll say yes. If you ask them about geography (at least until very recently), a lot of them will say, 'Mmh, I don't know.' And of course, that's an error. Geography isn't just an expression of the economy, it also forms the economy. The holy trinity attempts to suggest why this proposition makes scientific sense. So, I hope that there will be work that pushes it forward and makes it more operational. The people who have already made some progress in this direction are the evolutionary economists of technology. But it's up to us, really, to develop the tools and the analytical models and the measures and the evidence.

There are also the classical questions: what are the changes in patterns of location, in the specialization of cities, regions, and nations in the world economy, what are the resulting patterns of trade and economic development? My sense of it is that every social science discipline has things to contribute to those. But many of the essential questions of the 21st century are questions about geography, because they concern globalization (of goods, services, information and money), technological diffusion, and migration. And we have better tools for dealing with them than we used to. I think we now need a generation of rigorously-trained economic geographers who are able and willing to tackle them.

KLAUS TSCHIRA FOUNDATION

The Klaus Tschira Foundation gGmbH

Physicist Dr. h.c. Klaus Tschira established the *Klaus Tschira Foundation* in 1995 as a not-for-profit organization designed to support research in informatics, the natural sciences, and mathematics, as well as promotion of public understanding in these sciences. Klaus Tschira's commitment to this objective was honored in 1999 with the "Deutscher Stifterpreis" by the National Association of German Foundations. Klaus Tschira is a co-founder of the SAP AG in Walldorf, one of the world's leading companies in the software industry. After many years on the board of directors, Klaus Tschira is now a member of the company's supervisory board.

The Klaus Tschira Foundation (KTF) mainly provides support for research and student projects in applied informatics, the natural sciences, and mathematics, educational projects at public and private universities and selected projects dedicated to the preservation of historical monuments and the arts. In all its activities, KTF tries to foster public understanding for the sciences, mathematics, and informatics. The resources provided are largely used to fund projects initiated by the Foundation itself. To this end, it commissions research from institutions such as the *European Media Laboratory (EML),* founded by Klaus Tschira in 1997. The central objective of this institute of applied informatics is to develop new information processing systems in which the technology involved does not represent an obstacle in the perception of the user. In addition, the KTF invites applications for project funding, provided that the projects in questions are in line with the central concerns of the Foundation.

The home of the Foundation is the Villa Bosch in Heidelberg, the former residence of Nobel Prize laureate for chemistry Carl Bosch (1874-1940). Carl Bosch, scientist, engineer and businessman, entered BASF in 1899 as a chemist and later became its CEO in 1919. In 1925 he was additionally appointed CEO of the then newly created IG Farbenindustrie AG and in 1935 Bosch became chairman of the supervisory board of this large chemical company. In 1937 Bosch was elected president of the Kaiser Wilhelm Gesellschaft (later Max-Planck-Gesellschaft), the premier scientific society in Germany. In his works, Bosch combined chemical and technological knowledge at its best. Between 1908 and 1913, together with Paul Alwin Mittasch, he surmounted numerous problems in the industrial synthesis of ammonia, based on the process discovered earlier by Fritz Haber (Karlsruhe, Nobel Prize for Chemistry in 1918). The Haber-Bosch-Process, as it is known, quickly became and still is the most important process for the production of ammonia. Bosch's research also influenced high-pressure synthesis of other substances. He was awarded the Nobel Prize for Chemistry in 1931, together with Friedrich Bergius.

In 1922, BASF erected a spacious country mansion and ancillary buildings in Heidelberg-Schlierbach for its CEO Carl Bosch. The villa is situated in a small park on the hillside above the river Neckar and within walking distance from the famous Heidelberg Castle. As a fine example of the style and culture of the 1920's it is considered to be one of the most beautiful buildings in Heidelberg and placed under cultural heritage protection. After the end of World War II the Villa Bosch served as domicile for high ranking military staff of the United States Army. After that, a local enterprise used the villa for several years as its headquarters. In 1967 the Süddeutsche Rundfunk, a broadcasting company, established its Studio Heidelberg here. Klaus Tschira bought the Villa Bosch as a future home for his planned foundations towards the end of 1994 and started to have the villa restored, renovated and modernised. Since mid 1997 the Villa Bosch presents itself in new splendour, combining the historic ambience of the 1920's with the latest of infrastructure and technology and ready for new challenges. The former garage situated 300 m west of the villa now houses the Carl Bosch Museum Heidelberg, founded and managed by Gerda Tschira, which is dedicated to the memory of the Nobel laureate, his life and achievements.

Text: Klaus Tschira Foundation 2004

For further information contact:

Klaus Tschira Foundation gGmbH
Villa Bosch
Schloss-Wolfsbrunnenweg 33
D-69118 Heidelberg, Germany
Tel.: (49) 6221/533-101
Fax: (49) 6221/533-199
beate.spiegel@ktf.villa-bosch.de

Public relations:
Renate Ries
Tel.: (49) 6221/533-214
Fax: (49) 6221/533-198
renate.ries@ktf.villa-bosch.de

http://www.villa-bosch.de/

PHOTOGRAPHIC REPRESENTATIONS

Photographic representations: Hettner-Lecture 2003

Plate 1   Michael Storper in the *Alte Aula*.

Plate 2 & 3   Klaus Tschira and audience in the *Alte Aula*.

Plate 4 *Alte Aula*, University of Heidelberg.

Plate 5 Reception.

Plate 6 Reception.

Plate 7 Reception.

Plate 8 Internet transmission of second lecture, Department of Geography.

Plate 9 Outdoor talk in the departmental gardens.

Plate 10 Seminar in the studio of the *Villa Bosch*.

Plate 11 Debates in the historical gardens of the *Villa Bosch*.

Plate 12 Seminar presentation.

Plate 13 Michael Storper.

Plate 14 Seminar summary.

LIST OF PARTICIPANTS

List of participants

The following graduate students and young researchers participated in one or several of the three seminars with Michael Storper:

BAUR, Nicole; Department of Geography, Heidelberg
BELINA, Bernd; Department of Geography, Bremen
DALLGAHS, Ingo; Department of Geography, Jena
DECKERT, Jana; Department of Geography, Heidelberg
FEDERWISCH, Tobias; Department of Geography, Jena
FREYTAG, Tim; Department of Geography, Heidelberg
GENYING, Chang; Department of Geography, Heidelberg
HALDER, Gerhard; Department of Geography, Stuttgart
HENNIG, Thomas; Department of Geography, Marburg
HOYLER, Michael; Department of Geography, Heidelberg
IBERT, Oliver; Department of Geography, Bonn
JAKOBI, Akos; Department of Regional Geography, Eötvös Loránd University, Budapest
JÖNS, Heike; Department of Geography, Heidelberg
KISS, János; Department of Regional Geography, Eötvös Loránd University, Budapest
KLINGER, Thomas; Department of Geography, Trier
LOICHINGER, Elke; Department of Geography, Regensburg
MAGER, Christoph; Department of Geography, Heidelberg
MATTISSEK, Annika; Department of Geography, Heidelberg
MOßIG, Ivo; Department of Geography, Gießen
PÄTZOLD, Kathrin; Department of Geography, Humboldt-University, Berlin
RABE, Claudia; Department of Geography, Karlsruhe
SACHS, Klaus; Department of Geography, Heidelberg
SCHMID, Heiko; Department of Geography, Heidelberg
WILLMS, Ulrike; Department of Geography, Duisburg-Essen
WOLKERSDORFER, Günter; Department of Geography, Münster

Plate 15 Some participants of the Hettner-Lecture 2003.

Cover design: Tim Freytag and Volker Schniepp
All photographs in 'Photographic representations' by Heiko Balzerek

HETTNER-LECTURES

1 *Explorations in critical human geography* DEREK GREGORY 1997
2 *Power-geometries and the politics of space-time* DOREEN MASSEY 1998
3 *Struggles over geography: violence, freedom and development at the millennium* MICHAEL WATTS 1999
4 *Reinventing geopolitics: geographies of modern statehood* JOHN A. AGNEW 2000
5 *Science, space and hermeneutics* DAVID N. LIVINGSTONE 2001
6 *Geography, gender, and the workaday world* SUSAN HANSON 2002
7 *Institutions, incentives and communication in economic geography* MICHAEL STORPER 2003

Please order from: *Franz Steiner Verlag GmbH / www.steiner-verlag.de*
Distribution by Brockhaus / Commission, Kreidlerstraße 9, D-70806 Kornwestheim
E-Mail: bestell@brocom.de Tel. 0049 (0)7154 1327-0 Fax 0049 (0)7154 1327-13